UNTOLD UNTIL NOW: WORLD WAR II STORIES

DADDY AND OTHER HEROES

UNTOLD UNTIL NOW: WORLD WAR II STORIES
DADDY AND OTHER HEROES

KAREN BRANTLEY

Kroshka Books
Huntington, New York

Editorial Production: Susan Boriotti
Office Manager: Annette Hellinger
Graphics: Frank Grucci and Jennifer Lucas
Information Editor: Tatiana Shohov
Book Production: Patrick Davin, Cathy DeGregory, Donna Dennis, Jennifer Kuenzig, and Lynette Van Helden
Circulation: Lisa DiGangi and Michael Pazy Mino

Library of Congress Cataloging-in-Publication Data
Brantley, Karen
Untold until now: World War II stories, Daddy and other heroes / edited by Karen Brantley.
p. cm.
ISBN 1-56072-715-2
1. World War, 1939-1945 Personal narratives, American. 2. World War, 1939-1945—United States. I. Title.
D811.A2B72 1999 99-42769
940.54'8173—dc21 CIP
[B]

Kroshka Books, a division of Nova Science Publishers, Inc.
6080 Jericho Turnpike, Suite 207
Commack, New York 11725
Tele. 516-499-3103Fax 516-499-3146
e-mail: Novascience@earthlink.net, e-mail: Novascil@aol.com
Web Site: http://www.nexusworld.com/nova

Printed in the United States of America

In Memoriam

MY FATHER

OSCAR KENNETH BRANTLEY

BORN DECEMBER 1, 1923

DIED JANUARY 19, 1997

"OUR HERO"

The worthy cause-
A sigh, a pause...
Now sets the sun
On freedom won.
Just a job done,
A look back when begun...
Touch of red on the horizon,
The sun's almost gone.

Karen Brantley
December 26, 1998

inspired by my sister,
Nanette Brantley Greer

CONTENTS

Contents by Service

Merle Francis Peterson	U..S. Air Force, 340th Bombardment Group, Squadron 489
Otto Rahill	Fifteenth Air Force, 97th Bombardment Group, Squadron 414
Glenn H. Rojohn	Eighth Air Force, 100th Bombardment Group, Squadron 349
Leonard E. Rojohn	Eighth Air Force, 381st Bombardment Group, Squadron 585
Billie Joshua Seamans	Fifteenth Air Force, 301st Bombardment Group, Squadron 419
Robert Maier Smith	Seventh Army, 44th Infantry Division, 114th Regiment
Lal Duncan Threlkeld	U. S. Army, 95th Infantry Division, 15th Cavalry Regiment
Jack M. Williams	U. S. Navy, Torpedo Squadron Twenty-one
Cleo M. Willoughby	First Army, 45th Infantry Division
Dorris Wells Wilson	U. S. Navy, Second Gunnery Division
Haskell Wolff	First Army, 99th Infantry Division

PREFACE

A generation of men who fought for our freedom looks back at their lives; some with melancholy, some with unforgotten energy, and others with reluctance. World War II means something different to each man who served, yet a common and tightly woven thread binds their attitudes and senses of patriotism.

As these heroes who served on many different levels face an inevitable end, it seems a shame to let their memories of World War II die with them, unchronicled and forgotten. Not only do the men interviewed have their personal remembrances to share about that war, but their philosophies about life give insight to the kinds of men they are and the experiences that shaped their lives.

In my quest to document my father's stories of World War II, and also those of others, I took a seemingly endless ride on an emotional roller coaster. With each dear man, I found myself listening and responding much as I did when my own father talked to me. And in each one I saw the same kind of man as my father: thoughtful, loving, brave and successful. Memories of conversations with my own father flooded back time after time as I sought the company and stories of these courageous and endearing veterans of World War II. I left each interview with my heart full of pride and respect for such men as these.

The main consideration is this: when someone speaks to you, listen. Listen with your heart and soul. And memorize not only their words, but their facial expressions and the feelings conveyed in their eyes. Then forever you are bound to one another, and to another time gone by.

Karen Brantley
December 7, 1998

With appreciation
to my mother,
Lois Mahurin Brantley,
for the idea
and for her support

ABOUT THE AUTHOR

Originally from southeast Arkansas, Karen Brantley is a pharmacist currently living in Oklahoma City. She graduated from Northeast Louisiana University. Her interests include writing poetry, penning calligraphy, and the pursuit of genealogy. Her genealogical quests have earned her membership in the United States Daughters of the American Revolution and the United Daughters of the Confederacy. She is currently at work composing her second novel, a Southern saga.

Karen's first book began as an effort to document her father's World War II stories after his death. At her mother's bidding, she pursued the stories of other veterans, culminating with that of the pilot from her father's flight crew. The two men who felt as brothers toward one another during World War II never met again after the war. This book was written for the love and respect of her father, driven by patriotism and the need to preserve for posterity an anthology of valuable memories.

Introduction

I was the ultimate "Daddy's Girl." My daddy didn't take a step that I wasn't right there with him. When he was building something, I was there handing him the tools and asking too many questions as I watched the sweat roll down his face. When he was sleeping, I was curled up next to his back with one leg slung over him. When he ate his nightly bowl of ice cream while watching the late night news, I was up in the chair, squeezed in right next to him. When he was working on the police force, I waited up for him to come home. I would never go to bed until I knew Daddy was home. He looked so handsome and brave in that policeman's uniform. I can remember jumping into his arms just as he came in the door, and that he smelled of cigarette smoke and other policeman-type things. I always got to ride in the police car with Daddy during our small town parades down Main Street. We headed up the parade and I got to blow the siren.

Whatever Daddy thought was funny made me laugh, too. I love to remember his face lighting up with laughter over a good joke; the way he laughed from head to toe over a practical joke he played on one of our neighbors or my mother. Every year when we watched the "Miss America Pageant," Daddy hugged me and told me I was his little Miss America. He loved to have a good time and I loved being there with him.

He was the best dancer and taught my sister and me how to follow, letting him take the lead. Nothing was more pleasurable than seeing my mother and daddy dancing together. It was perfection. Dancing with Daddy was like floating on a cloud. He whispered instructions in my ear just before he would make the next dance move and it made me look like I knew what I was doing. I will never forget dancing in my daddy's arms. Those strong arms held me in so many different ways all my life. There were hugs of comfort, congratulations, pride, sorrow, happiness and many times "just because." He carried me when I was sick or asleep, he held back my long hair when I threw up, and he hugged me awake many mornings when I didn't want to get up and go to school.

He told me I could be anything in the world I wanted to be. Before I was born, there was a savings account established for my college education. With Daddy, it was never "if" you go to college but "when." As a child, I attended an unair-conditioned elementary school in the stifling heat of my southern hometown. Daddy brought a huge fan to my classroom and told the teacher it should follow me each year to my new room. We had the most comfortable classroom in the building, thanks to Daddy.

When I talked to my daddy, he looked me right in the eye and really *listened* to me. We had countless philosophical discussions. I loved to listen to him expound on his ideals, especially on the back porch swing. Whenever an old World War II movie was on television, I watched it with Daddy. Often, this would inspire him to tell his war stories. The only audience he had for these old war stories were his two daughters. We heard them many times and we always listened like we had never heard them before. He made us know what he experienced. He made his experience part of our lives, too. I am thankful for that and so much that Daddy gave to me all my life. He was my hero. And we never let each other down. My father, Oscar Kenneth "Kent" Brantley, died on January 19, 1997. I will never get used to being in this world without him. Within these pages are the war stories of Daddy and other heroes.

Karen Brantley
December 1, 1998

CHAPTER ONE

OSCAR KENNETH BRANTLEY

(1923-1997)

I registered for the draft in 1942 after graduating from Little Rock High School. I worked at the Arkansas Ordnance Plant in Jacksonville, Arkansas, as I waited for my call to duty. Later that year, a friend and I decided to join the merchant marines. We went downtown in Little Rock. Up and down the sidewalk there were recruiters with information about the army, the army air corps, and the merchant marines. The first place we came to was the army air corps. Something we saw there drew us in, and we walked through their doorway instead of going to the merchant marines. And that's how I came to be in the Eighth Air Force, 381st Bombardment Group, 585th Squadron. I was eighteen years old.

Basic training started November 1942 at Camp Robinson in Little Rock, Arkansas. I was sent to Purdue University, then I earned my Aerial Gunner Wings in Salt Lake City, Utah. I picked up my B-17 crew in Gulfport, Mississippi, May 1944, and in August we were sent to Ridgewell Field in England.

L.E.Rojohn, D.L.Chamberlain, V.E.Paul, T.D.Bandler,
O.K.Brantley, R.N.Schade(Replaced by Abbott), C.Yevtich, J.E.Williams,
M.L.Heatherington, J.F.Macknyk
GULFPORT, MISSISSIPPI ~ JUNE 1944 ~ CREW #4407

My first mission was on September 25, 1944, to Frankfurt, Germany. The B-17 planes and crews were assigned take-off and formation positions. It was understood among the crews that the last plane to take off probably wouldn't make it back to the base. The planes at the rear were usually the first to go down. In fact, it wasn't uncommon to see the bedding and foot lockers of those tail-end crewmen packed and set aside. It made room for the new crews coming in. I thought about whose bunk I must have taken when I first got there...the bunk recently slept in by a gunner or pilot or navigator who did not return after his mission.

Home Sweet Home
INSIDE THE B-17 F

Since it was our first mission, our crew was assigned to that last position on take-off, and also the last position in formation. We took off while it was still dark so that we would arrive over our target at daylight. And we made it back from that first mission without any problems, but the next thirty-four hours would not be as easy. Over the next three days we flew missions to Osnabruck, Cologne, and Magdeburg, Germany. When we got to Osnabruck, we discovered that the bomb bay doors would not open, but we were able to salvo the bombs. In Cologne, the bomb bay doors opened, but two of the bombs would not eject. I was told to kick out the live bombs. I remember looking down through the bomb bay's open doors at the far away countryside of Cologne. There was nothing between me and the ground but the bombs. I stood on a plank that was nothing more than a catwalk. I lowered myself down into the bomb bay area so that I could extend my leg toward each bomb, and bracing my other leg, holding on tight, I kicked, kicked, and kicked the two live bombs out of the plane. Somehow in the excitement of all that, I accidentally fired the guns and shot the aerial of the plane in half, which was quite embarrassing because the pilot and co-pilot thought we received a direct hit since the aerial was right over their heads. They were preparing to bail out! This really was something! We had to get rid of those live bombs or they would have exploded, taking us with them. And we could not risk returning to the base and landing with live bombs still on board.

In Magdeburg, we took accurate flak along both wing tips. It was almost impossible to take evasive action. Flak hit the plane's right wing. Then I almost lost consciousness when my oxygen hose became disconnected.

We had a three-day break after those three missions. Our down time was spent catching up on sleep, playing cards, playing golf, and going in to London. Then we were sent on a bombing raid to Kassel, Germany, where we received plenty of flak over the target. The lead navigator lost his way going back to the base. We found ourselves flying over the Ruhr Valley where we saw a large concentration of industry. This was one of the most dreaded spots on location to have to cross.

Our missions were eventually spaced to every other day. On our next mission to bomb Cologne, the soup was so thick we could hardly see, but there was little flak and it was an easy run. On our mission to Brux, Czechoslovakia, we flew in the lead squadron position and received plenty of flak which ruined our ship putting holes in two main tanks, as well as all over the plane. Two men on the crew were hit by flak. The navigator was hit above his left eye. On approaching the target, the bomb bay door malfunctioned. I hand-cranked them open. The next mission was Schweinfurt and it was easier. We considered those easy missions "milk runs."

I flew a total of thirty-five missions. We encountered various problems. As I said, sometimes the bomb bay doors would not open, or the bombs would not drop. There was always the danger of the plane or the crew getting hit by flak. I was all over the plane solving problems and sometimes I would actually get to fire the guns. We watched other planes from our squadron go down and would always try to count the number of parachutes. We saw some planes go down in flames and explode. The amount of antiaircraft fire seemed to escalate from mission to mission. One time the number three oil tank was hit by heavy flak and our plane caught fire on landing.

On our way to do some "good" bombing

On our nineteenth mission to Cologne, Germany, we taxied out to the runway and prepared for take-off. This was a short landing strip with trees at its end. The planes had to take off with precision or crash into the trees. We went over the check list and everything seemed in order to proceed. As flight engineer, I always stood between the pilot and co-pilot on take-off. I called off the ground speeds so the pilot would know when to pull back on the stick for lift-off. This time, when the pilot pulled back on the stick, it would not budge. If the plane did not go up, we were going to crash into the trees. We were right at the end of the runway when I saw that the pin through the stick had not been removed. Removal of the pin was necessary for the plane to lift. I dove down and removed the pin allowing the plane to elevate. We went right over the very tops of those trees. It was a close call.

On Christmas Eve 1944, a Sunday, we were scheduled to bomb Frankfurt, Germany. Our target was an airfield twenty miles north of Frankfurt at Ettinghausen. This was the greatest force of heavies ever flown on a single mission. It included two thousand heavy bombers and nine hundred fighters. The Frankfurt airfield was one of ten airfields to have over thirty-five hundred tons of bombs dropped on it during this massive bombing raid. Thirty-one bombers were lost on that mission. We had clear weather and could see the targets. The bombing was all good. This record bombing was called the Eighth Air Force's yule gift to the Nazis. We flew in on fumes to enjoy the next day's Christmas dinner of black beans.

The weather was freezing that January 1945. In fact, on one mission to bomb an airfield four miles from Cologne, we flew in temperature of fifty-six degrees below zero Celsius, taking off and landing in a snow storm. My thirty-first and longest mission was to Berlin on February 3, 1945. I flew with a different crew on this one. The pilot of this crew was Thornton. Other crew members were Quatrine, Peterson, Cochrane, Cohen, Borden, Klein, Chamberlin, and Mishalow. Flak made a hole in the nose of the plane and we could feel the vibrations of bursts of flak nearby. Klein lost consciousness when his mask froze up and he couldn't get oxygen. Borden, Cohen, and I applied first aid. We saw two planes collide and go down. One of the planes went down with the tail flip-flopping over the nose, another was burning as it fell, and another one exploded. This was our fifteenth and mightiest blow to Berlin. Nineteen of our bombers failed to return from this mission.

Another mission to Brux, Czechoslovakia was with my regular crew which had Leonard Rojohn of Pittsburgh, Pennsylvania, as pilot. It is one I will never forget. Our target was the oil works and we successfully bombed and destroyed the target. We were in heavy flak which caused our plane to suffer twenty-two holes, and the number four engine's cylinder to burst. The navigator was hit in the knee by flak. During the return to base, we ran out of gas and landed in Brussels, Belgium. We sought shelter in some barracks that only hours before was occupied by the German Luftwaffe. We decided to pool our resources. I was the only one who had money, so we stood in a circle and I divided it evenly among the crew. It's all each of us had to get by on until we could get back to base. We split up, some staying at the barracks, and some going into the city of Brussels. I ventured into the town of Zarentem. Walking down the street, I stopped at a curb. I felt a tug at my arm and looked down to see a small child. She stared at me and asked in broken English if I was from America. I told her I was and she invited me to come home with her. She let me know her family wanted to meet an American soldier. She took me by the hand and led me through the streets to her small home. When we arrived, she began to explain my identity to her parents who did not speak much English. The family seemed excited. They invited me to stay for dinner, and I did. The mother served bread and porridge with tea.

They wanted to hear about America and the American people. We took pictures together and I learned their names. Their last name was Moret. The parents were Herman and Marie-Lauise, and the daughters were Elisa and Alida. I will never forget their warmth and hospitality. It is one of my favorite memories from the war. After spending three days in Belgium, we returned to the air base in England with the 533rd Squadron Crew.

Alida, Elisa, Marie-Lauise, and Herman Moret
ZARENTEM, BELGIUM OCTOBER 1944

I feel the real heroes in World War II were the infantrymen. They suffered more on a daily basis than any others. They fought the war hand to hand. It was a tough life on the ground. The men in the air had it a little easier, that is, as long as they weren't shot down. I don't remember feeling afraid, and that's because I was so young. But there were plenty of scary moments. The older I've gotten, the less I want to get on an airplane. I figure I used up all my chances flying over the English Channel seventy times during the war.

When I returned home from the war, I wanted a career in law enforcement. I was an Arkansas State Policeman before settling in McGehee, Arkansas, where I was on the city police force. I wanted to make a difference in our community. I thought the place to begin making a difference was with the community's children, and I took an active part in the educational system through police programs associated with the schools. Subsequently, I served on the school board. Later, I left the police force to operate my own automobile business. It was a decision based on the desire to accumulate a stronger financial base. I always thought it was important to own property and to save for the future. This new business venture afforded me the opportunity to accomplish my goals and provide a better future for my family. It gave me independence, the same thing I had risked my life for in World War II. I never gave up the idea of serving my country and I tried to continue doing so after the war. I was the State Commander of the Veterans of Foreign Wars in Arkansas during 1963. Also, I served as president in Jaycees, the Lions Club, and was quartermaster for the American Legion. It's important to be an active volunteer in your community and I tried to exemplify that concept.

The best decision I made in my life was to marry a good woman. My wife, Lois Mahurin Brantley, has been a steady source of strength and support throughout our married life together. I knew the first time I saw her that she would be that kind of person. Once I met her, there was no one else for me!

I suppose if I would change anything about my life it would be to find a way to stay in law enforcement and make it worthwhile financially. It was the thing I loved to do and I have missed the association with police work. Looking back, maybe I should have gone to college and studied criminology. That's why I try to influence the younger generation to get all their education when it's available to them.

As the next to youngest of nine children, I just barely got here, but my life has been a good one. You won't hear me complain. You should know that the older you get, the faster time passes. Fifteen years can go by in the snap of your fingers. Don't let it leave you wondering about your accomplishments and what you might have done. Work hard and be somebody. When you are proud of yourself, then others are, too. If there is someone you admire, it may help to shape your life's goals. My mother, MaryEtta Cordrey Brantley, was one important influence in my life. She showed me by living example that one can do whatever he sets his mind to do. She never stopped short of inspiring me and helping me accomplish my goals. After the war, I began to accumulate rental property. It was my

O.K. Brantley

mother, at age sixty-five, who I depended on to go out and collect the rent. She was a remarkable woman who could do anything.

Another person I highly respected and admired was my World War II pilot, Leonard Rojohn. He seemed the ideal man to me. He was good-looking, intelligent, confident, and likeable. I knew he would be a success in his life. I came back from the war wanting to be like Rojohn.

A man has to put his family first. That's where you can have the most influence as a human being. It's very important to respect others, regardless of age. I tried to impress upon my daughters the idea of patriotism and independence. I told them they could do anything in life they wanted if they would focus. I told them to pick a star and never let it out of their sight.

Somewhere down the line, when people think of me, maybe they'll say I was a man whose word was dependable, who stood up for what he thought was right, who was successful, and a man who took care of his family and wanted to help others, too. Oh, yes, and one more thing, that I was not a quitter. That's one thing I always told my girls: "Don't be a quitter."

Chapter Two

Warren S. Bloch

December 20, 1998

I was born on September 19, 1920, in Offenburg, Baden, which is a small town nestled in the foothills of the Black Forest. I came to the United States from Germany in 1936, and lived with relatives who were my mother's cousins, a prominent family in Pittsburgh, Pennsylvania. I applied for citizenship in 1941, which was to become finalized in December. When the Japanese attacked Pearl Harbor on December 7, 1941, and war broke out, I was immediately declared an enemy alien. This disallowed my impending citizenship. Of all the people most anxious for the United States to become involved and victorious in this war, who more than I? An expelled Jewish German refugee!

My father served in World War I and considered himself a patriotic German. He had a vinegar factory. It was the most modern vinegar factory in southern Germany. He lost it within six months after Hitler took over. Hitler had enacted the Nuremberg Law which took the right to sue away from Jewish citizens. In 1933, when my father became a *persona non grata* in the Nazi era, the bank called in his business mortgage, which was money he had borrowed to modernize the vinegar factory. My father went to the former owners of the factory, and they agreed that they would ostensibly own the business, but retain my father to run the factory and make sales. Only a few months after this was arranged, he went to the office on a Monday morning and found himself locked out. As a Jew, he had no rights, so he couldn't do anything about it.

There were people in concentration camps even before I left Germany. My brother, Hans, tried to date a Gentile girl and was put in jail for a week. That was in 1935. Even as late as 1936, when my brother and I were preparing to leave Germany, people said to us, "Why are you leaving? This is going to blow over." Of course, we knew better. My parents came to the United States in May 1937, which was nine months after my brother and I arrived here.

In 1942, a friend advised me that based on intelligence, it was easier to get promoted in the navy than in the army. In the U.S. Navy enlistment office, they took all my credentials and afterwards sent me to an office where I was interviewed by a rather old and highly ranked naval officer. He asked me if I were born in this country. Meekly, I said, "No." It appeared that he did not hear me. He then asked if my parents were born here, and again I meekly said, "No." When he asked if my grandparents were born here, I replied, "No," and he heard me. So, he asked again if I were born here, or my parents. Finally, upon hearing me, he politely told me that he could not accept my application.

Within the year, I was drafted. Because we were now at war, it didn't matter about my citizenship. They wanted any man who could go. I was working and making fifteen dollars a week, giving eight dollars each week to my parents. My relatives did not want me to go because I was helping to support my parents financially. I went along with them about my draft deferral, but I didn't like this idea.

Eventually, I did go into the army. After being in the U.S. Army for almost a year, I was finally made a citizen of the United States. This took place in El Paso, Texas, in 1943. And this was when I changed my first name from Werner to Warren. Why I chose "Warren," I don't know, because I still cannot pronounce the "R."

I came from a country where I was persecuted. I felt a great sense of patriotism for the United States. I wanted to serve in the military and help win the war against Hitler and the Nazis. It felt great to be in the United States where I could live with all the amenities and go to a good school. So, how do you think I feel about this country?

When I arrived in 1936, Germany was acknowledged to be the most cultural country in the world. All the great scientists and architects were from there. The Germans put on a show with their precision marching and it all looked very powerful. The United States was a multiracial, multisocial democracy. At first, by comparison, I thought the U.S. was backward. Everyone seemed to be arguing among themselves. Then in 1941, when Roosevelt said we needed a two-ocean navy, I saw how the United States could get things done. In order to accomplish this, we had to increase the capacity for production of steel. As I rode through Homestead, Pennsylvania, on my way to work, I began to notice that the U.S. Steel company had grown to three or four times its regular size. This happened in only a few months. It was incredible! Steel began rolling out of the mill before too long. I changed my mind about this being such a backward country. I thought, "Hey, they've got something on the ball."

In the army, when there were maneuvers, or whatever was called for, the Americans...some Italian, some Greek, some Indian, some native Indian, some Jewish, all different kinds of people from New York to Los Angeles...the Americans were ready. I could never see any problems in the army. The means of communications was so perfect, and the execution was so perfect. I was amazed! I had never seen anything like that in Germany. Everybody knew where Hitler was going to end up. Rommel said when we landed in Africa and overwhelmed him, "How can I cope with all the equipment they have?" The United States had all the supplies and had them right in place. We had the production capability far superior to the Germans whose productions were being destroyed day in and day out by our bombers. When you think about our B-17s filling up the skies over Europe...How could anybody fight that sort of thing? This country had the nerve and the ability, and despite its multinationalism, it had patriotism. And it still does today! If we are called upon to do the right thing, we will do it.

After I was drafted, I was taken to an induction camp in Fort Mead, Maryland, where I was classified. I was given an intelligence test and a mechanical aptitude test. I came out high on both of them. I was put into antiaircraft, which at that time was part of the coast guard. They trained me in clerical school because I knew how to type. I remember the sergeant telling me on the first day, "Everything you learned about typing, forget it. We are going to teach you how to type." In a few weeks, I went from typing sixty words per minute, to one hundred-ten words per minute. If you keep your eyes and ears open, you can learn from anybody. Typing did not put me in a subordinate position. It was a means of communicating. The faster I could type, the faster I could communicate. It served me well all my life.

One of my duties was as the stenographer in courts martial. They had courts martial all the time because some soldiers went AWOL, or got drunk off the base...One case I remember was when a captain was being court-martialed because he took gasoline from the company reservoir to put in his car. He was driving GIs into Los Angeles. I think I was among them one time.

Major Graves was my commandant. He and I had a really professional rapport. He told me what to do. I did it. No comments. No friction either way. It was absolutely fantastic. One time he told me that even though our roster didn't allow but for one sergeant, that he was going to make me a sergeant anyway. And he did. I stayed in the 820th Antiaircraft Battalion until they decided no more antiaircraft units were needed. When we were disbanded in 1944, the men from our unit were sent overseas to the infantry. Major Graves said he wasn't going to let me go into the infantry. A person with the rank of sergeant had to do in the infantry what was required of a sergeant. What does a former antiaircraft man know about leading the infantry? We had no training for it. We heard back from our men who went over to Italy. Different ones lost arms, legs; were decapitated, killed...trying to serve as a sergeant in the infantry and having had no training for it. Eventually, Major Graves succeeded in getting me into the medical corps.

I went overseas with the 134th Evacuation Hospital. There were a number of medical units on the troop ship. Most of the people on board were seasick, except me. I was a great seafarer. It was a crazy ride from New York to Le Havre. One day was hot; the next bitter cold. We zigzagged across the Atlantic. The various officers of different outfits were fighting among themselves. As we approached Le Havre, France, there was arguing about how our units would be transported to the camp. Our captain did not want our unit transported by cattle truck, but by train. His argument was that our unit had nurses and it was better for them to be on the train. But he lost.

We arrived about three o'clock in the morning at Le Havre. Our unit, nurses and all, loaded onto the trucks and it took us about two hours to get to Camp Chesterfield. The other outfits loaded onto the train. Soon after we arrived, we got a call to rush down to Dieppe where a French saboteur had run the train into a cul-de-sac at the station. Many people from our medical units were killed. Our hospital was set up immediately and the wounded were brought to us. The evac-hospital was trained to set up within hours. I worked in surgery preparing the surgical packs, and we went right to work. We were able to save some of the lives. Our unit was awarded a citation for this. The outfit performed heroically.

We were at Chesterfield for about a week, and later we were in Belgium where we treated many men who were wounded at the Battle of the Bulge. We were inundated; working day and night. This was in January and February 1945. The men had been wounded in December 1944, and transported from field station to field station until finally getting to our evac-hospital. They were all in bad shape. It was terrible. Our team performed miracles.

In April 1945, the day after Roosevelt died, we traveled from Belgium into northern Germany. I felt proud and happy to return to Germany as an American G.I. for I had no rapport with the German people. I had nothing but disgust for those people. Some Jews will say, "Where was God in the 1930s when He didn't take care of the Jews?" I say, "Where was God in the 1930s that He made animals of the non-Jewish European citizens?" These people were all guilty of inhuman behavior. Hitler defiled the Europeans.

All I wanted to do was get out of Germany so that I could get home to support my parents. I managed to pass the warrant officer's examination, but I could not find an outfit that needed one, which was the only way to get that rank. A month after V-J Day, my outfit was sent to Arles, near Marseilles. At Marseilles, there was talk of sending us to the South Pacific, or perhaps back home, or somewhere else. Eventually, I was sent to Indiantown Gap, Pennsylvania. I was discharged by early 1946.

When I came back from the war, I went back into the same office where I had worked before. This was a chain of furniture stores. I worked in the main accounting office. They had gotten along without me during the three years I was away, and when I came back I was treated like an intruder. I went to the owner, Mr. Ohringer, and told him he should fire me because I wasn't needed. He asked me if I had the combination to the safe. I told him I didn't. He told me to go back to the office, and I did. One of the ladies in the office came to me and said, "Here's the combination to the safe." From that point on, my presence in that office was entirely different. Now everyone knew that the owner favored me, and that I could go to him anytime I had complaints.

Warren S. Bloch

With the help of the G. I. Bill of Rights, I took a cram course for the CPA exam in 1949. I passed it. I continued working for the furniture company. In 1957, it was taken over by new owners. In 1962, I decided to give them only morning hours so that in the afternoons I could develop my

CPA practice from my home office. When they went bankrupt in 1964, I was well positioned to be a full-time CPA, which I am still doing.

I live for the sake of change. Every moment of my day, I ask myself if there is anything I can do differently that will be faster or more efficient. I'm talking about my business, not my home. I am not so handy at home!

* * *

As an observer of history, my heroes are Roosevelt, Truman, and Eisenhower. I always have had a keen desire to study and be a worthy citizen. There is nothing I would change about my life; anything else would be wishful thinking.

I am a deeply religious person, although I don't ostentatiously practice religion. I believe in the Ten Commandments and in the practice of good ethics. I have no special wish about how I would like to be remembered. Whatever good I'm doing in this world, I hope when I pass away it will be remembered and appreciated by the people who knew me.

As far as its government is concerned, as far as its people's lives are concerned, there is no country that compares to the United States for its tolerance and the way we get along with each other. I think it's remarkable. World War II brought that out, there's no doubt about it. Just as the Civil War tore us apart, World War II brought us together.

CHAPTER THREE

HILBURN OLIVER BORLAND

NOVEMBER 21, 1998

Before I joined the army, I went to National Defense School in Memphis, Tennessee, to learn how to work on airplane engines. After two months, I enlisted in the United States Army on October 9, 1941. I had just turned twenty-one years old at the time. From my home in Pickens, Arkansas, I went to Camp Robinson in Little Rock, Arkansas. It was during the World Series, when at Camp Robinson we lined up in front of a hut and were told to undress, bend over, spread our cheeks, piss in a bottle, and go three doors down. Outside, we were sworn into the army. I said goodbye to my mother, boarded a train in Little Rock, and didn't see her again until January 2, 1945.

A buddy and I considered going to Officers Candidate School. He went, but I changed my mind when I found out that the second lieutenant had the shortest life span of anyone in the infantry. That certainly helped me make a decision. I did not even apply.

I was sent to Jefferson Barracks, Saint Louis, Missouri, where I had to take an I.Q. test to get in the U.S. Army Air Corps. From there, I was sent to Keesler Field, Mississippi for nine weeks training. This course of training had been a year's course before the war broke out. I was in training to be an airplane mechanic. Ours was the second class to graduate from Keesler Field. The first graduating class was kept as instructors. In my class, men with last names from “A” to “H” were sent overseas. The rest of the men were kept as instructors. The third graduating class was sent to gunnery school.

I was assigned to the 394th Bombardment Squadron (H), Fifth Bombardment Group, in the Thirteenth Air Force. We did not receive any basic training. They gave us a 30-06 bolt action Springfield rifle which we kept under out cots, except during guard duty. We had B-17 and B-18 planes in our squadron. The B-18s were later replaced by all B-17s. Our squadron trained combat crews. We called ourselves “The Bomber Barons.” I left San Francisco on the USS Coolidge, stopping in Hawaii. It was December 20, 1942, when I crossed the international date line.

I was in engineering as an assistant crew chief. My duties included keeping the planes inspected and in shape for flying. My crew specialized in maintenance of mechanics. We replaced the engines after they had flown a certain number of hours. There was nothing glamorous about being on the ground crew. It was pretty much the same, day after day. But much depended on us doing a good job. We suffered all kinds of disappointments and hardships. We were either baked by the hot jungle sun, or drenched by the tropical rains. Often we lacked in equipment and parts, and had to improvise. We scavenged many a junk pile. Also, we were capable of stealing from another plane in order to fix the one we were working on. It was easy at times to become disheartened and disillusioned. We moved from jungle island to jungle island. Many of us were transformed from bright young boys to weary old men. But we continued to make our best effort to get those bombers in the air.

Our planes were sent to Midway before the Battle of Midway, and we were in that battle. After Midway, I was sent to Veti Lavu, Fiji, where our planes flew search missions. We arrived in Fiji on Christmas 1942. Joe E. Brown came there to entertain us. They had a drink on Fiji called kava. I never tried it, but I was told if you drank enough of it, it would paralyze you. Supposedly, the Fijians made the kava by chewing up the raw roots and spitting it in a pot.

From Fiji, I went to Guadalcanal on a C-47 transport plane. On June 16, we came into Guadalcanal during a 102-plane Japanese air attack. Two B-25s came to fly cover, as we left to fly around below treetop levels over another island for about an hour. The pilots were seeing how close they could get to the water. We got so close that the propeller was picking up spray off the water. When we finally landed, there was water running out from under the tail wheel of our plane. I sure was glad to get back on the ground. I saw two ships beached and burning in the harbor. The Japs lost one hundred planes that day. It was their last daylight raid on the canal. After that they sent over a few betties, Japanese bombers, every night for harassment. We called them "Washing Machine Charleys." The Japanese made two planes sound like a whole squadron of planes by having them fly at different pitches and different speeds.

We made us a type of scarecrow and used a Japanese skull for the head. It had a real Jap helmet on it, too. We called him "Washing Machine Charley." Eventually, our commanding officer made us take him down.

We were bombed quite a bit. My first night on Guadalcanal, there was a bombing attack. We didn't even have time to dig a foxhole. We tried to get in a bomb shelter with some other guys, but they wouldn't let us in. They told us to go find our own place. We went over and got in an open pit where they were in the process of building a communications center. They bombed us off and on through that night, and we lost some men from our squadron. The next day we got up and dug ourselves a hole. We cut down coconut logs to cover it with. I think that cover was about ten logs high.

We were on the equator. If you got off the road, you were in the jungle. I went two years without seeing a white woman, and very few native women. We had water purifiers so we could drink the river water. The water tasted like chlorine; even the coffee tasted like chlorine. We slept in tents with cots. If we were anywhere long enough, a week or two, we'd find boards and get our tents up off the ground. We hung mosquito netting across the front opening. We got pretty good at making ourselves a place to live. Our food had to be brought in by ship. Mostly we got dehydrated foods like eggs and potatoes. At six-foot-two, I started out weighing one hundred-eighty pounds, and lost down to one hundred-sixty. Some of that food you just could not eat. We wore as little clothing as possible. Mostly we went around shirtless in our britches.

One time on Guadalcanal, a B-24 landed with the hydraulics shot out. The flight crew stopped it by having the waist gunners hang their parachutes out the side windows to slow it down. We were told that was the first time something like that happened. A Jeep was on the landing strip to meet them, but when the plane veered to the right, it hit the Jeep. Nobody got hurt that time. And I saw lots of belly landings, some of which were pretty serious.

They had to do this when the landing gear wouldn't come down. Even if one gear would come down, the pilot usually would rather belly land.

One of our planes on Guadalcanal was a B-24 called "Pretty Prairie Flower." Our commanding officer, Colonel Marion D. Unruh, from Pretty Prairie, Kansas, flew it. My best friend, Gillis, was the tail gunner on it. Gillis was a sergeant from Pennsylvania and went through the Battle of Guadalcanal in the infantry. Later on, he transferred to the air corps. As a mechanic, he was a good welder. He told me stories about his experiences in the infantry, and we became close friends. Sergeant Gillis and Colonel Unruh built a platform and put a gunner turret in it. They rigged it up to shoot water from the guns. This was so they could learn out how to swivel it around and shoot. They used it for practice.

We had the first radar plane. It had three 100-pound bombs in the bomb bay. On approaching the target, Colonel Unruh would hold back the squadron while he went over the target and dropped one bomb. He'd watch where it went, then if he was satisfied, he'd let the squadron fly across.

On December 30, 1943, the "Pretty Prairie Flower" was seriously damaged and Colonel Unruh had to land. He let them know the island where he was landing. Pictures were taken of him and his crew waving from the east beach of New Ireland where they landed safely. Emergency rations were dropped and a submarine went in that night to try to rescue them, but there were Japanese across the island and they captured Colonel Unruh and his crew. The colonel and another officer were taken as prisoners, but undoubtedly, they executed my friend, Gillis. When this news arrived, morale in the group slumped. Colonel Unruh had endeared himself to all his men. The New Year's celebration was quiet and solemn. Colonel Unruh had flown one hundred-two missions. It was rumored he made it back from the war, only to be killed later on while flying experimental planes.

We always watched on the horizon for the return of the planes. Finally, we'd see the specks appear. Those planes didn't fly much faster than a crop duster. We would start counting the planes as the specks flew closer. I remember the day we were watching and counting as we realized Colonel Unruh's plane was missing. After that day, when Colonel Unruh and Gillis didn't come back, I never let myself get close to another flight crew. It was just too much if they didn't make it back.

At Christmas time on Guadalcanal, I decided I wanted a Christmas tree. I couldn't get anybody else to go along with the idea. So, I went out in the jungle by myself and found a tree and brought it back. I started putting it up and everybody around began helping me. They pretty much took over. We decorated it with just anything we could find to put on it. We put on some cotton to look like snow, some wadded up tin foil, and then made a star to put on its top. Many of the men came by to have their picture made with my Christmas tree, which was in front of the tent where I lived. Our Christmas dinner was C-rations made into a soup, and Spam cooked a special way.

We had a chapel there, and an American cemetery. One of the men I knew from back home was buried there. His name was Tommy Lewis, a Marine, who was the brother of a local dentist. And we had entertainers come to Guadalcanal with the USO troops. One of them was Ray Bolger who later played the scarecrow in "The Wizard of Oz." We had movies to watch while we were there. We watched them outdoors sitting on coconut logs.

* * *

Next we went to Los Negros in the Admiralty Islands. The bunker our plane was in had about three thousand dead Japanese behind it, all pushed into one great pile. If you would have known any one of them, you could have recognized him. At the time, we made jokes about it because we didn't feel sorry for them. The only good Jap was a dead Jap. I think we were just trying to laugh it off. We just couldn't dwell on it. I thought it was their fault I had to be there. More than a month later, we left those dead Japs just as we found them when we took off for Wadke Island near New Guinea. Having seen all those dead bodies affects me more now than it did then. Here lately, I think more about it.

While I was there, I saw someone from home. It was E.C. Freeman who was serving in the Seventy-second Squadron. He and his buddies had "something" to drink. They set a whole fifth of cherry brandy down in front of me, and I drank the whole fifth. I stumbled all the way back to my outfit. To this day, he still likes to tell that story on me if he gets the chance. At first, we never got any alcohol to drink. Then later we were occasionally provided with a quart of Australian lager beer or some kind of New Zealand beer that we couldn't drink. Toward the end, they gave us two cans of beer each week. If someone didn't want to drink his, he could sell it for a premium.

Wadke Island was a half mile wide and one mile long. While on Wadke Island, I became sick with arthritis and was flown to a hospital in New Guinea. I was told it was something I'd just have to learn to live with. I stayed in the hospital for three weeks, then hitched a ride back to Wadke Island on a mail packet tug boat, which was skippered by a guy from Arkansas.

The Japanese put out propaganda leaflets. One of them was a type of ticket that showed an American G.I. holding up a baby, supposedly conceived and born during his absence, with his wife looking at the two of them. Printed on it was: Ticket To Meet Your Wife and Kid. On the back it said, "Here's all you do: 1.) Come towards our lines waving a white flag! 2.) Strap your gun over your left shoulder, muzzle down and pointed behind you. 3.) Show this picture to the sentry. 4.) Any number of you may surrender with this one ticket." Then below was written: "Japanese Army Headquarters."

We were about three hundred men over strength, partly because they didn't want to send back the experienced mechanics. Some of the combat crews were sent to Australia for a week of rest, when most of us hadn't been out of the jungles in over two years. When they came back, they brought a bunch of steaks with them. They were cooking the steaks at the mess hall. We hadn't had anything to eat for a long time, not anything to speak of. For us, eating had become an unpleasant necessity. A couple hundred of us were standing around there watching, and one of the men picked up a piece of coral rock and threw it at the mess hall. The rest of the men did the same thing. It sounded like a hail storm. That was all that really happened. The next day the Inspector General came by and found we were just short of armed mutiny. That's when they began to send some of us on rest leave, and some back to the States. I was in one of the groups that got to go back home. That was in October 1944. I was in New Guinea for about two months during the invasion of the Philippines because they might have needed the troop ship we would be sent back on in case the invasion failed. I got to see part of the invasion fleet before we left. After we boarded the liberty ship, we saw an ambulance pull up to the dock. They started unloading a bunch of men in on stretchers. We found out later they were "Section Eights." These were men with mental trouble. When these men came up on deck to exercise or get some fresh air, we stood in groups to make sure they didn't jump overboard. About half the passengers on this trip home were the "Section

Eights." Some had battle fatigue and probably never should have been in the army. It took us twenty-one days to get back to the United States, and we arrived on Christmas Eve. As we approached San Francisco, one of the mental patients broke a glass over a light bulb and killed himself with it. They buried him at sea just two days out of San Francisco. There wasn't even anyone to play taps for him.

* * *

After the war, I stayed in South Carolina for a while. I managed a flower and seed store. I married there and began my family. My daddy wanted me to come back to Arkansas, so eventually I did. He wanted to send me to pharmacy school and open up a drug store. When I first got back to Arkansas, I didn't know what I was going to do. I managed to get by on drawing my 52-20 from the government, which meant twenty dollars a week for fifty-two weeks until you got a job. My brother had a dairy, and I could have gone to work for him. I went to the saw mill and applied for an office job. Right after that, Mr. R. A. Pickens offered me a job working on the Pickens Farm. He hired me as a handyman, but I ended up managing the mechanics shop for the next forty years. Even though there's a lot of difference between airplane and tractor engines, it was still what I knew best. I retired in 1986.

Certainly, being in the war influenced my life. I wouldn't have been a mechanic if I hadn't gotten the training in the service. I never minded getting my hands greasy. I always liked mechanic work. I enjoyed overhauling an engine and hearing it run afterward.

There are two heroes in my life. I consider both Colonel Unruh and Sergeant Gillis heroes. They both gave all they had to give. Each already had all his missions in and could have come home. Gillis didn't like just sitting around, and volunteered for that last mission he got shot down on, even though he had already done his fifty. Each of them wanted to make sure the job got done. Colonel Unruh was a man who had no fear.

I had patriotism before I went into the service. I never will forget when we were at Jefferson Barracks in Missouri and we had retreat, to hear taps played brought tears to my eyes. I was just proud to be an American. And

Hilburn Oliver Borland

when we rode the train heading west, at Lincoln, Nebraska, the people were so nice to us. They came out to the train and gave us candy, magazines, and postcards. That was patriotism. I've always been a patriot, so although I didn't really want to be in the army, I didn't mind serving. Patriotism is the love of country; to go out and do something to help your country, instead of asking your country to help you. I define patriotism in my heart because that's where I feel it. We were taught patriotism at school when I was little. We sang patriotic songs in school and learned things that would make us become better patriots. We don't need wars to teach patriotism. We need to be taught young enough to make us want to be patriots. Today, our education system ought to look at what the schools were doing in the 1920s and 1930s that taught children patriotism. We need to practice those same things in the schools nowadays. The way it is now, you can't say a prayer in school. And I don't hear children singing those patriotic songs like we sang. Teaching patriotism to our children has to come from their homes and schools. I always tried to live a life in front of my children that could guide them. I think I did a pretty good job on both my sons. I must have done something right. I want my life to be remembered as being a good father and a good husband. If you can be that, the rest of it will take care of itself.

I'm sure everybody has things they would change in their lives if they could. But you can't. You just have to be satisfied with life. For myself, being in the service taught me how to better live through difficult times. Even now, that type of training is needed in my life.

I've wondered why I came back alive when so many didn't. It's something that can't be explained. Some people don't realize that the men in close combat weren't just fighting to be patriotic, but for their buddies. They fought for their own survival, but also to help save their friends. That's what was in their minds at the time they were actually fighting. We think of those who didn't make it when we wonder about these things. You can't pick out a hero by saying a person looks like one; the smallest man can be the biggest hero when it comes right down to it. A hero's not born, he's made.

Chapter Four

Robert Edwin Boulware

August 14, 1998

I was nineteen years old, and I was in the Fifteenth Air Force, Second Bomb Group, Ninety-sixth Bomb Squadron. It was 5:30 a.m. in Foggia, Italy, on July 16, 1944. When we got ready to take off, Lieutenant Huntington, our bombardier, became ill and couldn't go. Lieutenant Arthur E. Cox volunteered to take his place. This would have been Lieutenant Cox's last mission.

It was my fifth trip over Vienna, Austria. We flew up there without too much difficulty. We didn't see any fighter planes, but when we got to the target, there was flak- you could almost walk on it, it was just black. They were shooting every gun they had.

We were flying in number four position. For some reason, the lead plane didn't drop its bombs, nor the two behind it. But Cox went ahead and dropped ours. And the planes behind us dropped their bombs.

The colonel in the lead plane said we were going back over. It was our second time over that we got hit. The bombardier, Arthur E. Cox, who was from Chicago said, "We're still in flak. It's a wonderful day in Chicago." Then we got a direct hit. It blew the nose off the plane and blew Lieutenant Cox to pieces. The plane went up in the air, turned over on its back, and went into a spin. We were at 24,000 feet. While the plane was spinning, we couldn't move or do anything. The pilot put the plane on automatic pilot and it righted itself. Then they hit us again with antiaircraft fire right under the number three engine where the co-pilot, Lawrence Jenkins, was sitting, and it blew him out of his seat, breaking his legs. He was thrown back in the floor on the side where it was burning. I was back in the tail all this time. I was checking engines and reporting to the pilot what was on fire and what was throwing parts out. When that number three engine was hit, communications went out on the airplane. That's when the pilot and navigator decided it was time to leave, and they bailed out. They didn't know where Jenkins was. They thought he'd already bailed out, but he'd fallen into the bomb bay. Although the bomb bay doors were closed, they were supposed to open up on one hundred pounds. But they didn't. Jenkins couldn't stand up and was lying down in the bomb bay. Ray Voss, the waist gunner, opened up the door to the radio room to find it empty. The radio operator had already bailed out the back door. The lower ball gunner, Owen Bruce, was the first one out.

I was in the tail and when the plane went into a spin, all my ammunition fell on me. I was trying to rake it off me and get out of the tail. I had always promised Bruce that I would make sure he got out of that lower ball. If we lost power, then the lower ball had to be rolled up by hand, otherwise he'd be left out in the open, and he didn't have a parachute because there wasn't room to wear one in the lower ball. I didn't wear a parachute either. I had a chest pack that I laid to one side because wearing it made it impossible to fire the guns. The only ones who actually wore their parachutes were the pilot and co-pilot. Theirs was a seat pack, so they sat on their parachutes. Their seats were made for that.

Anyway, Voss, after seeing there wasn't anyone in the radio room, opened the door that went to the bomb bay. (This all happened in seconds.) It was smoky and he couldn't see anything, so he opened up the pilot's door and found fire coming out of everywhere. He slammed the door shut, and then heard someone yelling at him. He looked down in the bomb bay and saw Jenkins. We all had big, heavy suits on and couldn't recognize each other, so he didn't know who it was. In the middle of the smoke and fire, Voss reached down for Jenkins, but he couldn't pull him up. Jenkins tried to tell him to open the bomb bay doors, but Voss couldn't. Being a waist gunner, it wasn't something Voss was expected to know how to do.

In the meantime, I crawled out of the tail and up to the lower ball to find it open and empty. There wasn't anyone at all in the back of the plane. I went on through the radio room, and then I saw Voss, although I didn't know who he was for sure. We had oxygen masks on, hats, and big heated flying suits.

We couldn't talk, so we were communicating with gestures. He was trying to find out how to open the bomb bay doors. I was the armor on the plane. My job was to secure the bombs and arm them, so I knew more about the bomb bay area. I signalled him it was up on his left. He hit it, and as I was standing there, whoosh, those two were gone... out the bomb bay doors! The minute the doors opened, Voss jumped right along with Jenkins. But I didn't jump, and I have no idea why. I was on the plane for twenty-seven miles after everyone else had bailed out. The plane was on fire and going down, as I calmly walked on to the waist door, took off my flak suit, and bailed out. I didn't look back. I had never bailed out before. There had been no practice. I wouldn't have jumped, except that I had to. If I could have gotten up front to the cockpit, I would have tried to fly the plane since I was trained to do so in the event that the pilot or co-pilot couldn't.

As I threw out my arms and legs, it seemed I stopped completely. It was as if I could just lie on my back or do whatever I wanted. There was no sensation of falling. It seemed everything else was moving around me, but that's not what was happening- I was going down! It was the most peaceful thing on earth, no sound. It was a wonderful thing, a feeling I'll never forget. I felt as free as anything. I didn't know my altitude, so I wasn't going to pull my parachute, but I went into a cloud and I didn't know where the ground was, so I went ahead and pulled it. I was probably 5,000 feet in the air. When I pulled my chute, I passed out. I remember hearing the slight rustle of the silk as it came out. That was the only sound. There was dead silence up there. I had waited long enough to jump that I was far away from the fighting. I had wanted to wait until I was right on the ground, hoping the Germans wouldn't be able to spot me by my parachute and shoot at me. One of our P-51 fighters spotted me and followed me, circling me, all the way down. He kept everybody off me until I hit the ground. Then he waved his wings and he was off.

A funny thing was that I'd laid my chute to the side while we were on the plane, and I didn't know it had gotten shot up. It was right next to me and bullets were going everywhere. It was full of holes. They were really light parachutes and I weighed only about one hundred twenty-two pounds. I began falling at one hundred miles per hour, then after the chute opened I fell at fifty miles per hour. It didn't seem I was really falling. I was thinking something was wrong because the ground didn't seem closer. I didn't think I was going down. Suddenly I could see power lines and telephone poles, so I guided away from those. I began to get ready to land, but it was too late, I'd already hit! I landed in a potato field.

I'd already unstrapped my legs, so when I hit, I took off my harness and started running. But the Germans had seen me coming down and had followed me in their car. There was no time to bury my parachute or anything. There were some Free French prisoners working in the field and they got to me first and started hitting me over the head, trying to find whatever I might have on me, like my escape kit. The Germans captured me within a few minutes with their guns drawn. The first thing they did was take my heated flight suit. There were three of them and they were pilots. They weren't bad to me, in fact, they were real nice. They seemed more like comrades, probably because they were Austrian Germans and not hard-core.

I'd been armed. We were told if we went down very far inside enemy lines to destroy everything we had on us, just throw it away. I'd already thrown out my gun and my knife. I had an escape kit on me. This was the escape kit issued to the men flying out of Italy over Yugoslavia. I was told it contained maps, a compass, and ten thousand dollars in gold seal American currency, although I never checked the contents of that kit. The gold seal money wasn't available in the United States, and it wasn't good in the United States. It was special currency identical to our usual money, but with a gold seal on it. If the Germans would have gotten hold of that money, the Americans would have honored it. We had it because they wanted us to buy our way out from behind enemy lines if we went down in Yugoslavia instead of preying upon the citizens. Also in my kit was some morphine to use if one of our people got critically injured. We'd "take-the-out" with the morphine. Each of us had one morphine injection in his escape kit. We also had orders that if somebody was critically injured to bail him out, because we couldn't help them up there. If somebody got hit by flak, it tore him up and he'd probably bleed to death.

I was dressed in my uniform, although I wasn't supposed to be. We were supposed to wear plain shirts and pants under our flight suits, but I didn't because I hadn't planned on going down. The first thing the Germans wanted to know was how I got shot down. All their fighter planes were there with them setting under the trees because we'd blown up their airport. I thought this might be a good time to lie. So, when they asked if the German fighter planes shot me down, I said, "Yeah....," even though it was flak that brought us down. I hadn't even seen a fighter plane. I told them what I thought they wanted to hear.

When my plane went down, the Germans told me it came down like a ball of fire. Because it was on automatic pilot, it landed itself even though it was on fire. It set a field on fire. They thought I was the only one who had escaped. They told me I was lucky, that I was the only one who got out of that plane. I didn't tell them I had ridden it twenty-seven miles after everyone else got out. I just said, "Oh, that's terrible. That's too bad." At that time, I didn't know that the bombardier had been killed. All I knew was that I had checked to make sure there was no one else on that airplane before I bailed out.

They gave me something to drink and a cigarette, then took me down to the train station and put a guard with me. We got on the train. He could speak no English; I no German. We just grunted at each other. He wasn't particularly threatening, but he let me know he'd shoot me if I tried to run.

We had not dropped one bomb in the city of Vienna. We blew up all the railroad tracks, the roads, the bridges, everything around the town. But not one bomb was dropped in the historical city. So, we couldn't get into Vienna because the railroad tracks had been blown up. We had to get off the train and walk into Vienna. I had no intention of trying to get away. The civilians were just as dangerous as the soldiers. They were just as likely, if not more, to kill you if you tried to escape. We got over there, and this soldier guarding me, who must not have been very smart, let me know he needed to go to the restroom. He indicated for me to stay put. But I got to thinking about it and decided it might be a long trip ahead of us and maybe I'd better go, too. So, I went around to the other side and went in. When he came out, I was gone. When I came out, I watched him running up and down the street looking for me. Finally, I said, "Hey!," and he had the most relieved look on his face when he saw me. Then I was put on a streetcar. Most of the women I saw around there had on white silk blouses. They were made from our white silk parachutes! None made any remarks toward me.

Then I was taken to a prison that was about a thousand years old. They walked me down and threw me in a cell. Pretty soon I heard somebody say, "I told you he'd be here." It was my pilot. I was told Jenkins had been captured and taken to a hospital because of his legs. The rest of the crew was all there. Everybody from my plane had made it, except for Cox. Most of them thought I hadn't gotten out of it. All eight of us were in the same cell.

The next morning they put us all on a train and they separated us. I stayed with the lower ball gunner, Bruce. I went to Frankfurt-on-the-Main.

There I was interrogated. I'd been told I wasn't to say anything but my name, rank, and serial number. I wasn't supposed to talk to these people. If you didn't say what they wanted you to, they'd punch you with their bayonet and cut you up, or beat you on the head, or take you out and shoot you. I mean, they know how to interrogate people. But I was bullheaded and wasn't going to let them do me this way. One of their sergeants was interrogating me. He wanted to know what plane I was flying in. I answered that I didn't know. He said, "What do you mean you don't know?" I continued with, "I don't know." He said, "Well, you saw what you got in, didn't you?," and I said that I hadn't, that it was dark and I couldn't see. He was writing all this stuff down. He got upset with me and had me thrown back into the dungeon. This was where they'd dug out places under the railroad station. It had a straw bed against the wall and there was only enough room to stand beside it. The room was only as long as the bed. This was all underground. There was no light or anything, and they just threw me in there. They were single cells. You couldn't see anybody; they didn't want you to. If you had to go to the restroom, they'd wait until no one else was in sight to let you go. It was solitary confinement. The guard would not talk to you. We had bread and water- one piece of bread and one cup of water each day passed through an opening. It was dark, heavy bread, and that's what kept us alive. I think it had sawdust in it. At first, I wouldn't eat it. It tasted terrible. But it got to where it didn't taste too bad. When we were marching, you could take a string and tie it around a piece of that dark bread and hang it from your waist, and it could rain all day and that bread wouldn't get wet. It was tough stuff.

I was beat up, sore from the fall and everything else. I went to sleep and slept for two days. Then they took me out to the captain. He told me they had looked at my papers and decided I was not from the air force, that I had never flown in a plane before, that I was a spy, and they were going to shoot me.

When I was back in Italy, I'd had my picture taken dressed in peasant clothes, an old suit with an old, long tie on. I was instructed to turn over this picture if I was captured by the underground. This was always a possibility as we flew over Yugoslavia and Greece. I had forgotten all about this picture and they had taken it from me, using it to declare that I was a spy. They told me they would give me a chance. There were some things they wanted to know. They said I could tell them or they'd take me out and shoot me. They had three guards standing there with rifles. I said, "I guess you're gonna have to shoot me." They got up and marched me out into the woods, and I thought I was going to get shot. I really did. I didn't say anything, and they didn't say anything. They just stood me up out there; didn't blindfold me. Then they went over and began talking to each other and smoking a cigarette. I was thinking I was in a horrible jam. I thought I was going to get killed, and there wasn't any need in getting excited about it. They finally decided to take me on back, without a word.

I knew what they wanted. They wanted to know how we were arming our bombs. Some of our bombs would be armed to go off when they hit the ground, but some were armed with delayed action. When we'd drop the bombs, say on a factory, some would go off immediately, then just when their fire trucks were arriving, more bombs would go off and get them, too. They wanted to know what time in the morning we were taking off, and what size bombs we were dropping.

I was in solitary confinement for twenty-one days. Then I was sent to Wetzlar, Germany. It was a kind of summer home where they kept you for one or two weeks, and they treated you pretty good. I got quite a bit to eat while there. But before I got out, they called one of their majors to interrogate me. Now, I'd been bayoneted, and hit on the head, and threatened with shooting...everything terrible. That major was just sitting up there and said, "Helloooooo, Mr. Boulware, how are you?" I answered, "Fine, I guess." He asked me if I was hungry. I just stood there and looked at him. He told someone to get me some bread and honey and a glass of milk. I ate, and he asked if I wanted some more. Then he offered me a cigarette and I took it. I sat there smoking, thinking, "What's going on here?" The major started laughing. He said he knew what I was thinking, but that he wasn't going to ask me any questions. He said he didn't need to ask me anything because he knew everything there was to know about me.

Then he asked me if I knew where the Biltmore Hotel was in Oklahoma City. He said he used to stay there. And he was speaking perfect English. Nice guy. He asked me if I knew where the theater downtown was, and told me he was an actor. He'd been an actor in a German theater group since 1934. They'd been to the United States in 1937 and 1938, and he was spying on Tinker Air Force Base in Oklahoma City. He told me not to be too upset about it. He said I didn't have anything to worry about now because I was a prisoner and the war was over for me, that I had it made. He said he was the one who still had to worry about getting killed. He pulled out a picture of his brother. In the picture, his brother had on a Texas A and M football uniform. He said his brother was still in Texas. And he had pictures of himself with American girls at Miami Beach nightclubs in Florida.

The major reminded me that I'd previously told the sergeant that I just wanted to come over there to kill Germans. That I'd volunteered to do it. Then he revealed that he knew I'd been drafted. I'd told them I wasn't married, but the major knew differently. And he knew when I had gotten married. He knew all the details of my military record. He even knew the score of my cadet exam. He told me everything right down the line. Everything.

I began to think how I'd been in solitary confinement longer than the rest of the other guys. They'd got out real quick. I decided they must have told all this. Right away, I was mad at my whole group because I figured they'd told it. I'd kept my mouth shut and got beat up for it. I accused them, but they denied it. After that, I got real careful about who I talked to, even my own crew. Then the gunners were all sent to Stalag Luft Four. That's where I stayed the longest. The officers were sent elsewhere.

Sometimes we'd have to march for as long as five days. In all, we marched over eight hundred miles. We never changed clothes or bathed. Sometimes we'd go five days without food or water. We'd had to leave our camp because the Russians were coming, and the Germans wanted to keep us prisoners. That's why they kept marching us down the road. It was wintertime and snow was on the ground. I never saw a fire the whole time I was out there. When you're cold all the time, I guess you get used to it. I was sick with dysentery and I was weak, but I never had a bad cold. Or maybe I had one and didn't know it. We ate charcoal, burnt wood, for the dysentery. Some men died from pneumonia. There were no medications.

The Germans had run out of gasoline and had to use mules to pull their cannons. They ran the mules to death. When one of the mules would fall, the Germans would cut his throat. Then we'd come along and take the mule. That was the only meat we had. They allowed us to have it because they wanted to keep going and didn't have time for that mule. They just left us out there in no man's land. They didn't care what happened to us. There were many farms where we were marching. They had big kettles out in their yards, as big as a kitchen table, and hundreds of gallons of stuff could be cooked in them. They could make a stew by putting in the mule meat, water, and a few potatoes. That's how we got the mule cooked. I ate mule only once or twice. Most of the time we ate soup that we were told was spinach, but I thought it was grass. It looked like grass and it tasted like grass. One time I stole a pack of cowfeed. As a farm boy, I'd tasted cowfeed before, and thought it would be something we could eat. I was so proud of what I had and was showing it off. I didn't know then that the Germans had ground up hay in the bran to keep us from eating it. But we ate it anyway. It didn't digest very well. But if you're hungry enough, you'll eat anything.

* * *

When they took us off the train to go to the camp, we had to march almost a mile. There was a redheaded captain who was crazy. He was always screaming. I never knew what he was saying. They had dogs and bayonets. They started running us, three hundred seventy-five of us, and when the ones in front would stop, we'd all pile up. That's when they'd bayonet us and then sic the dogs on us. I had about twelve bayonet wounds; another guy had seventy-five.

The radio operator in our crew was someone I hated. He was a "bad bill" collector from New York, about six years older than me. He'd try to tell me what to do. He was obnoxious. He was about six foot-three inches tall, and weighed over two hundred pounds. The dogs, for some reason or another, wouldn't bite me, but they really went after that radio operator. One of the dogs was about to tear his leg off. I thought that was really funny.

As we were on the road marching, we were put in a barn and guarded. The redheaded captain and the other German officers were in the town in a house, with the guards guarding us at the barn. Eight English tanks came up. When the tanks rolled up, the guards threw their guns down. We ran over and picked up the guns. The men in the tanks said the war was over. They'd pulled so far into enemy territory, and now they had to go back. They told us we could stay put until the army advanced far enough, or do whatever we wanted to do. Five of us took off for the town to capture the two German officers we were after. We did not take the radio operator from our crew with us.

That redheaded crazy guy, who was a captain over the other guards, was the meanest of all. And there was another one we despised. We went to the house in town where the German officers were. We found them and killed two of them. The redheaded captain was one of them. We thought he didn't deserve to be shot, so two of us held him and another took the butt end of a rifle and knocked his head off. That's the way he was killed. I didn't do the actual killing, but I was in on it. I was all in favor of it.

I found out later that he bayoneted us because his wife and two children were killed the night before in a bombing raid, and we were all bombers dropping the bombs. War's a terrible thing and I've thought about that since then, but at that time I didn't know. All I knew at the time was that we'd been bayoneted and treated terrible.

After we took care of our business in town, I went out on the road and used a submachine gun I'd picked up to stop the first car that came by. I told the driver to get out and start running or I'd kill him. He was a German captain, and he was driving a Jaguar with Red Cross signs all over it. Of course, we weren't supposed to interfere with anything that was involved with the Red Cross. He kept saying, "Red Cross, Red Cross," and I said, "Can't read. Sorry." I told him he had two choices: start running or be killed. I told him it didn't matter to me. And it didn't. So, he started running. We tore the signs off the Jaguar, got in it, and drove off down the road. That's how we got loose.

We headed for the front line. We got lost a couple of times. Once we found ourselves in the path of the Russians. They were bad soldiers. They were killing and raping all along the way. They didn't have any of their own weapons, just what they picked up along the way. We'd stopped at a farm house and used our guns to demand food. At this house there were two women and two children. They were going crazy when they knew the Russians were coming. Our group went outside. Two Russians came up to us, and one went back to get his buddies. We had a fire fight and we killed all of them. Then we got in the car and we left.

We got off to the side of the road when we knew the Americans were coming. After they arrived, we showed ourselves and said we were prisoners. They took us to the general's tent and gave us something to eat. The general said they had to keep moving and he wasn't sure what to do with us. He asked if our car was running all right, and said to go ahead in the car to Hamburg and try to get to Le Havre, France.

When we got to Hamburg, we went to the airport. A C-47 which was hauling gasoline came in. We talked to the pilot and told him we needed to go to Le Havre. He said he was in Hamburg every other night and would really like to have our car. So, the deal was made. We traded our Jaguar for a flight to Le Havre. We got out on our own with no help from anyone. We were dangerous, dangerous people. We'd had enough. We were going to get out, and we didn't care who we had to kill to do it. We had decided.

I was interrogated at Le Havre when I was first liberated. When I got there, they deloused us. I had on the same clothes from January until May, never had them off, never even had a bath. I just wasn't human. I'd slept in barns and ditches. They kept me there for two weeks until I weighed 130 pounds. They fed me six meals a day. They had us under barbed wire- we didn't go anywhere or do anything. They just fed us and talked to us.

Then we were sent by ship to New York City. All I had on was army issue pants and shirt. No hat. No tie. I didn't have anything to prove who I was. They processed us there and said they were sending all the Oklahomans to Arkansas. They asked how much money I wanted. I told them one hundred dollars. So, we got on the train. At the first town where we stopped, there was an ice cream vendor. I got off the train and told him I wanted some ice cream. He asked how much. I said whatever it is, I want it all. I bought all he had, took it back on the train, and we ate it. That's just how stupid we were. I think it cost me about ten dollars.

I'd never been a drinker. I was too young to begin with, and I was from a dry state. Then when we were flying, we couldn't drink. But I was planning on celebrating when I got home. I planned to tie one on. When we got to Saint Louis, I went into the train station and found a drug store that sold liquor. First, I asked them to sell me a suitcase. Then I asked them to fill it up with whiskey. I was carrying this heavy suitcase full of whiskey when two military police stopped me. They didn't believe who I was because of the way I was dressed. When I explained I'd been a prisoner of war, they asked me, "What's that?" Finally, they allowed me to continue, but they followed me to my train and said when I got back on, not to dare get off.

From Arkansas, I took the bus home. No one in my family knew I was coming. I went to where my wife worked and called for her to come down. When they told her that her husband was downstairs, she started crying. She didn't believe them. She told them I would have called her first. But I didn't. She came flying down to where I was and straight into my arms. I wanted us to get a big room at the hotel because I knew all my relatives would want to come see me. We got a room at the Biltmore and called everyone to come there. Then we went across the street to Beverly's to eat. When we got back to our room, everyone was there. They'd found the whiskey and were having a great time. I never got any of the whiskey that night. I gave away several bottles to my uncles since they couldn't buy it in Oklahoma. The next day I said I was still planning to get drunk. When I looked in the suitcase, it was empty!

Then, I went on convalescent leave down in Miami, Florida. I was seen by several psychiatrists. I took all my tests over. They told me I was crazy, but I was the kind of crazy they liked! They told me all that stuff wasn't bothering me and that it hadn't affected me because I was just doing what I thought I had to do. I was told I was in pretty good shape. They told me by the time I was thirty-five years old I would probably be all crippled up with arthritis from living ten months on the ground, and not having anything to eat, malnutrition. I only weighed seventy-two pounds when I got out on May 7, 1945. I was assured that after being a prisoner, I would never have to fight again: once a prisoner, never a prisoner again. But their plan was to send me to Japan to be on a B-29 squadron. I was supposed to be boosted in rank all the time I was in prison, but I never got that. The American government lied to us about the whole thing.

Five days after showing up to go to Japan, the war ended, so I didn't have to go. I was offered a discharge or to be admitted to the hospital for thirty days, at the end of which time, the government would decide if I got a pension. I took the discharge!

I began to have attacks of malaria fever after I got back home. When I went to the Veterans Administration Hospital, I couldn't get treatment. There was hardly any facility. For a while, the V.A. Hospital was located in some barracks out at the airport. They tried to tell me I had never been in the service because they couldn't find my records. But as soon as Korea broke out, I got notice to show up in San Antonio! Two hours before I was to leave for San Antonio, I got a call not to come because they'd called too many reserves and didn't have any place to put them.

Most of the stuff we went through in the war, we didn't want to talk about when we got back because people weren't interested. They wanted to forget all about it because it was over with. And we did, too. A lot of the our stories, the average person wouldn't believe. They don't take into consideration that a bunch of kids, nineteen and twenty years old with no sense, are over there fighting. The reason they're there is because if they're told to go out there and do something, then they do it. I never believed I would ever be shot down; I never even worried about it even though I'd see B-17s going down everyday, with men being killed and everything else. It never dawned on me it was going to happen to me. And then when it did happen, I was sitting there thinking, "This can't be; they can't shoot this B-17 down!" They had to prove it to me. I guess that's why I was the last man out.

* * *

Some of our kids may not understand patriotism. These kids nowadays have got it rough, in a way. They don't have the home life we had. What we call the good old days weren't really all that good, but those times molded people better than now. When I was a kid, I only knew of one or two killings that happened where I was from; but today, with television, kids are exposed to news that tells them of multiple killings in a single day. Of course, because of the war, my own exposure increased big time. When you give a guy a gun and sic the enemy on him, he becomes patriotic. He will fight. Most of the guys' thoughts were to "get him before he gets me" in order to survive. I think people are more patriotic now than they used to be.

America's not perfect. It's up to each of us to vote when we're supposed to, stand up for things, and make it a better place. Although our country may be terrible in many ways, it's still better than anything that anybody's ever devised so far. There's no other country even close to ours. If you ever went to other countries, you'd find out that our country's the greatest. It didn't get that way by people not being patriotic. People have been willing to give their lives. Wars have kept this country from going under. You must be prepared to die to stay free. A person who really wants to stay free is willing to fight and die for it. The hardest thing in the world for me to understand is people who don't want to be free. When you're free, you don't let anyone do anything except what you want done. It's called independence.

War was a horrible experience, and being a prisoner was a horrible experience, but there's nothing so bad that you don't get some good out of it. It made me have more compassion for people than I used to have. And I can't stand for anything or anybody to be hungry. When people are down and out, I try to help them. I've thought about whether I would want to

Robert Edwin Boulware

change anything about my life, and I don't think I really would. If I would change it, it might not have been as good, or better. I had a wonderful marriage for fifty-three years. My wife and I were buddies. We did everything together and we enjoyed each other. I have a son I'm crazy about-he's a real good boy. I've been blessed. I don't think I'd change anything. I don't feel like I've been mistreated in this life. My life wasn't a planned one. I just fell into it. And it all worked out well. I just hope people will remember me as honest and fair to everybody.

CHAPTER FIVE

LOUIS BURRELL, JR.

DECEMBER 12, 1998

I was born on December 13, 1917, in Manchester, Texas. My family moved to Idabel, Oklahoma, when I was one month old. I was working on my family's farm when I was drafted into the service on January 13, 1942. I was twenty-four years old and the youngest of five children. It was after the attack on Pearl Harbor that they started calling us in. The war was rough then.

I didn't want to go. Some of my friends had volunteered early, but I always said they'd have to call me to get me. It really got my mother for her baby to be called to the war. When I left for the service, my mother weighed 317 pounds. When I returned home from the war, she had lost 200 pounds.

I didn't know what branch of service I was going in, but I was put in a special group. From Fort Sill, Oklahoma, I was sent to Tuskegee, Alabama, and that's where we received our training. After basic training, we had specialty training. My specialty training was in ordnance armory- handling guns, ammunition, and bombs. My company was attached to the 332nd Fighter Group, a unit of black men. We were an all-negro fighting group. One famous squadron of that group was the Ninety-ninth Pursuit Squadron. These were the Tuskegee Airmen. It was thought that the black men didn't have the education, intelligence, and desire for combat required to be first-class fighter pilots. Under the leadership of Lieutenant Colonel Benjamin O.

Davis, Jr., this was proved wrong. We got the chance, and I was very proud. Our record of success speaks for itself.

I went through the eighth grade in school; never graduated. In the service, I was given an aptitude or I.Q. test. The first test they gave me, I made 113. I was told with my limited education that my score was a mistake. They made me take the test again, and the second time I scored 114. The group I was put in required at least a high school education. I was told that not even any of the flying officers had an I.Q. score as high as mine. So, I got in without being a high school graduate. I'm a good listener and that's why I pick things up. That's how I made it. I was lucky because this kept me off the front line, where most of my friends had to go. And many of them didn't come back. I was glad to be in a group way behind the front line so I didn't have to go out and fight. When some of those guys came off the front line, you couldn't even tell what they were... matted hair, muddy... it was terrible. You couldn't even tell what color they were. They looked like a groundhog or something.

We went overseas on the USS Levi Woodsbury, leaving from Virginia. They briefed us as we boarded the ship. As we got on, the captain asked us, "What are you going overseas for?" All they guys answered, "I'm going over there to fight for my country!" But when he asked me, I said, "To come back."

Those were some scary times, dangerous times. It took us twenty-nine days to get to Italy, and we had to fight our way over there. There were five hundred men on our ship, and a large amount of T.N.T. We were guarded by destroyers to protect us from enemy submarines, and we also had airplane escorts. At least two enemy submarines were intercepted and destroyed. When the submarines were detected, the horns on the ship began blowing, and all the destroyers came together and surrounded our ship. It was terrible, but it was exciting. What shook me up was what happened after we got to Italy.

It was January 1944. We landed and unloaded in Taranto, which was already bombed to the ground. We had to step over human arms with the skin still on them, and we saw skulls with the hair still on them. Everything was a rubble of stones from the bombing, and there was snow on the ground. We pitched our tents on the side of a mountain, putting down rocks and logs below the tents. The snow on the mountain kept a steady stream of water running below our tent at all times.

In Taranto, our first mission was to take out a German factory located underground where airplanes and tanks were being built. We had a time getting that thing out of there. It was called the Anzio beachhead. The bombing went on for months and months. In six months, we changed bases three times. After Taranto, we went to Salerno, and then to Naples. Naples is the most beautiful place I've ever been. It was never bombed. It had the most beautiful buildings. Finally, we worked out of Marseilles, France. I was in Europe for twenty-two months. I came home in October 1945.

* * *

Ours was a fighter squadron. When the fighter planes would go out strafing, firing their guns, it was my job to keep those guns working and loaded. Our fighter planes handled up to 500-pound bombs. We started out with the P-40 fighter, then the P-39, and the P-47. The last one we used was the P-51, the Mustang. That was the "bad" one. It had the speed. Our fighters took care of the bombers. When the heavy bombers would go on maneuvers, our fighters would go to protect them, shooting down the Germans. We had thirty-six planes ready to go at all times.

Some of our fighters were shot down and never made it back. Some got back shot up and crash landed. Sometimes they made it back, only to die on crash landing the plane. Each pilot had a sight which was located right above his head, and when the plane crashed, this sight would burst his head open. My armory group was the first to get to a crashed airplane, but we had to wait forty-five minutes to make sure the plane didn't catch fire. A fire truck waited with us. Then after forty-five minutes, we could get on the plane to discharge the guns. That's when we found the pilots dead of their head injuries.

The thing that really did get me is...you have to be pretty strong to stand a lot of that stuff...one evening we were standing in line at the mess hall, waiting to eat. One of our pilots had engine trouble and when he was trying to land, he crashed not too far from where we were, right by the mess hall. His plane caught afire. We couldn't do anything about it because the fire was too hot. We had to watch him burn up, the skin peeling back from his head so we could see his white skull. It was really nerve-racking. And we had to see it, our co-worker was burning up, and we couldn't do anything about it. The fire trucks put out the fire, but it was too late. He was already gone.

Early in the morning and late in the evening, you could look for those Germans to come around. We dug foxholes to protect ourselves and take away the shock of the bombs they dropped on us. Then we hoped the shooting and shrapnel would go over us. Digging that foxhole was always the first thing to do when we got to a new place. And we had just a little shovel to do it with. That ground over there was clay dirt. Hard ground. We had one guy from Louisiana who said he wasn't going to be digging a hole in that hard dirt, but the first raid we had he was worse than a gopher going after it! He went in there with that little shovel! Those foxholes saved many of our lives. If the bomb didn't hit you, it would shake you to death unless you were down in one of those foxholes. Mainly, the Germans were trying to bomb the airplanes at our airport in the early morning or late evening when we were sleeping. The airport was about a half mile from where we slept. If we didn't want to get messed up, we had to wake up and get down in the foxholes. Most of the time, we had four fighter pilots in airplanes ready to go, two airplanes at each end of the runway. When the radar picked up the Germans coming at us, our fighters would take off and intercept them, shooting them down and keeping them back.

It rained a lot the first six months we were overseas. We got our food in the chow line. All the food was together in a tin dish, and we kept pouring the water off it as we tried to eat. The dish had a cover on it, but of course, you couldn't eat with the cover down, so when you put it up, the food got rained on. We always had potatoes, sometimes beans, and sometimes spaghetti. They fed us pretty good. We were issued a quart of water a day to use however we wanted. We could drink it or bathe with it. I always drank mine. It was about two months before we ever changed clothes. It was tough.

We were allowed to write home. I wrote to my parents but wasn't supposed to say exactly where I was overseas. It was called "free mail" because all we had to do was write "free" on it for the postage. Our letters were censured. If there was anything in there they didn't want people to know, they cut it out. My mother told me later she got letters from me with holes in the middle where parts had been cut.

I went up in one of the planes only one time, and that's when it was time to come home. I had to fly then. It was for forty-five minutes just to get to the ship. And I wouldn't have done that if I had any other way to get there. I never liked the idea of flying in an airplane.

* * *

I think ours was one of the best groups in the world. I never saw so much cooperation in my life as working with those guys. There was a guy named Abbott Prowell who was smart, but had to beg to get in the service because he had bad feet and they didn't think he could be a pilot. They let him in, though, and he was one of our best pilots. And he was one of my best friends. He was a nice guy, and he could drive that airplane! When Lieutenant Colonel Davis would fly, Prowell was one of his escorts. Prowell's flying buddy was Joseph D. Ellsbury. One day when they were escorting Colonel Davis, they shot down seven German airplanes. Whenever the fighters fired their guns, it also triggered a camera, which showed their hits. That way we got to see what they had done. The pictures showed the planes on fire and going down in the ocean. That kept us going. Our fighter pilots never lost a bomber. Nobody ever shot down a bomber when our guys were with them.

One time Prowell's plane got shot up, lost a wing, and fell in the ocean. Another fighter called for help and circled him as long as he could, but finally had to leave before he ran out of gas. By the time the boat got to him, Prowell had drowned. I'll never forget it.

If I ever had a hero, it was Colonel Benjamin O. Davis, Jr., our commander. He wouldn't just send the guys, he went with them. Sometimes I felt afraid for him. Even though he was almost too tall to fly those planes, he would go with the guys. His plane was kept so polished, it was easy to tell it from everybody else's plane. It looked like a star, it was so bright and shiny. He had one rough time when his canopy got shot off and he had to come in without it. Other than that, Prowell and Ellsbury always kept him protected. Colonel Davis was all business. If you were a good soldier, you could get anything from him you wanted; if you weren't, then you had trouble. The colonel was a fine guy, and was awarded the Silver Star. Thanks to his leadership, the 332nd was awarded the Distinguished Unit Citation, cited by the Fifteenth Air Force.

Being in World War II was a good experience for me and influenced my life. When I got back from the service, eventually I went to work for Tinker Air Force Base where I worked until I retired. It was the training and education I got from being in the service that got me that job. And knowing a

Louis Burrell, Jr.

man like Colonel Davis influenced my life. He was a fair man who stood for discipline and all the right things. I've tried to be that same kind of man.

One thing I enjoy most is working with the younger people at our church. It's a good thing to talk to them and let them know things. I tell it to them straight. It might make them mad at me, but maybe later they'll understand and come around.

All my life, I was afraid of trouble. My dad taught us to stay out of trouble. He never allowed us to tell a lie. That burned him up. He said if we told him the truth we might get by, but for sure we wouldn't if we lied. And I can tell you, I've never been arrested in my life...maybe a few traffic tickets! But I've never been in any kind of trouble. I learned that from home, and I took it into the service with me. Daddy always told us, "Don't try to be like anybody else. Do what you can do, and be the best you can be." Those were his exact words, and I can say it's worked for me.

Chapter Six

Philip T. Cascio

August 2, 1998

It was the first part of the war. I was in the Eighth Air Force, the 303rd Bombardment Group (H), Squadron 358, known as Hell's Angels. We went down over Lorient, France, during our sixteenth mission to Saint Nazaire on February 16, 1943. Our plane was named the Spook. Only three out of ten got out of our plane. One who didn't make it was Captain Lawrence George Dunnica from Guthrie, Oklahoma. He was our pilot. He couldn't see that well, and he was our pilot! He really could not see. Hell, at the first part of the war, they'd take anybody! When I came back home, his mother and sister came to our home in Leland, Mississippi, where I was living with my parents to find out the true story about what had happened. I can remember seeing him trying to get out of the cock pit. He was either all shot up and couldn't get out, or maybe his boot got caught. He was about three-fourths of the way out of the plane when it went down. His mother wanted to know. And I can remember that night, I didn't want to tell her. But my uncle was there, and he said to go ahead and tell her because that's the reason she came. So, one thing lead to another and finally I told her. That night after we were in our bedrooms, I could hear her crying. It still makes me emotional....

We were on our way back to England and were close to the coast line. But we broke out of our mission to help another bomber who was straggling and had a bunch of ME-109 German fighters on him. We were young then and real energetic. Dunnica called out over the intercom, "Do y'all want to go down and help?" We were all full of vinegar and said, "Let's go!" So we went down to help. They were way below us. We made a circle around the plane. They were at about 5,000 feet and we were at about 20,000 feet. They had about five ME-109s on them. They were being shot up and about to go down completely. As we made the circle, the whole damn world came to an end. The German fighters started in on us. Now there were about fifteen of them. The other plane went down. We were trying to get back to Molesworth, England. We were about halfway over the English Channel. We had three engines shot out. The fourth was barely running. We crashed into the water. We sort of bounced on the water and that's when the plane broke half in two. We were about twenty miles from the English coast.

I was in the lower ball turret. When the waist gunners shot their guns, the clips would fall into the tracks and sometimes prevent the lower ball turret from going around. I'd only be able to go up or down. That's how I was able to get out before it jammed up completely.

I saw we were over the top of the water and getting ready to crash. Everything was dazed for a while. When I got out, I ran into the center piece of the plane and braced myself against the back wall of the radio room. When we hit the water, my back absorbed a lot of the shock. When we finally stopped, the plane started sinking. I ran into the radio room where there was a hatch on top and started trying to get out of the hatch.

The co-pilot, Orson E. Pacey, and the gunner, Harry W. Tucker, got out. The other fellows had blood all over the plane. You can imagine them being shot up with as many planes as we had shooting at us. I can even sometimes hear the ping of the bullets going through the fuselage of the plane. With all that stuff going on, I was lucky to be able to get to the hatch. The radio man was all shot up. He had blood all over him. I tried to help him, but I couldn't. We were sinking, so it was a question of our very survival, of taking care of each ourselves. I finally got out of the plane. I was lucky. We were all just so darned scared. When we were all trying to get out of the plane, I didn't want to be a fraidy-cat and get out first. I tried to help the radio operator out of the plane. I did my best to help him get out of that thing. But he was hurt very badly and told me to go on. He knew he couldn't make it himself. He was completely shot up and had blood all over him. His wife wrote me a letter years later wanting to know about it. That was about the most worthwhile thing I did...trying to get him out of that radio room. If he'd have gotten out, maybe I would have made a name for myself. But I didn't get him out, so I did not.

We had two rubber dinghies on the side of the plane. One of the dinghies was all shot up and sunk into the water. We were just lucky that one was untouched. I guess the man upstairs knew we needed a way out and fixed it up for us. The three of us got into the rubber dinghy. And you could hear the others either hollering or screaming or whatever it was. That was the part I had to tell Dunnica's mother, that he was trying to get out of the plane and couldn't. That he got stuck.

After we were in the water, the Germans passed by us about three times. They strafed us each time they came back by. We were in the water and couldn't do damage to anybody anyway. And we were already shot up. We stayed out in the water from one o'clock in the afternoon until four o'clock in the morning. Dark. Cold. You can imagine a February in the English Channel. We'd sometimes be so high in the air and looking down that, I don't know if it was imagination or what, I still say we saw two or three masts of a ship or something that was sunk back in the past. The masts of the ship were on the bottom and we'd be way on top of the waves, and I'm talking about so high that you could look down and see a ship's mast below you. I'm sure I saw that once or twice. And, like I say, we stayed out there for a length of time that was about fourteen hours. I was soaking wet and cold and all of that. We were just lucky we were able to hold on. We floated to the tip of France near Brest. Of course, nobody was there waiting on us. It was night time and cold. We couldn't walk after being in the water that length of time. You just can't move, that's all. We crawled from the dinghy onto the land. We saw a little shack off in the distance. So, we crawled all the way to the road and into the place to try to warm up and get out of the weather. It was about one hundred yards. We covered up with leaves over our soaking wet clothes trying to get warm. We stayed like that for about three hours. We slept. When we woke up we tried to find somebody to help us out.

We went to a French house. We gave them our uniforms which was real good stuff, leather on the outside and wool on the inside, our flight suits. They gave us French clothes in exchange. Of course, you know they came out ahead by far. They were scared the Germans would catch them feeding us, giving us something warm. They would holler, "Allemagne," and we could understand that meant Germans were in the vicinity. They wanted to help, but they couldn't help us, and they let us know to get the hell out of there. But before we left, they did give us some coffee which was made from the roots of the trees. They would burn the roots and make coffee out of it. They also gave us some dark brown bread which was a real change for us compared to the white bread we were used to. One of their bread loaves weighed about five pounds. It was filled with potato peelings all ground up and anything else they could put into a loaf of bread.

We wanted to go back and get in their barn, but they wouldn't let us do it. They kept hollering "Allemagne" and making the motion for "rifle." It was so dark and cold. We started walking. We walked for maybe a couple or three hours trying to find somebody to help us. Then, finally, all at one time, we could hear somebody hollering, "Halt!" There were Germans scattered all the way around us. I imagine they'd found our rubber boat. We'd tried to cut the boat and let it sink, but under our circumstances we didn't have the equipment.

So, we were captured by the Germans. There must have been about eight of them. From there they took us to their little hut. They let us sleep for about four hours. We were exhausted. After that, they put us on a truck and took us to Paris which was about two hundred miles away. We were taken to the Bastille. We stayed locked up there for some time. When they put me in that cell, I lost track of time. It was dark. I had no contact with anybody. Each cell was about twenty feet high, and three feet by nine feet long. When they slammed that door, I thought the world had come to an end. I was only twenty-four years old.

We must have stayed there about four days. They were breaking our morale. They would interrogate us. They'd take us into rooms and ask a thousand questions. They wanted us to tell them what we knew. But, hell, they knew more than we did! You'd be surprised how many of those Germans had come back from the United States. I remember one in particular who was from Gulfport, Mississippi. He asked me questions about places where I was from and mentioned names of people he thought probably I knew.

I thought about home. We were scared as we could be. Each of us was in a cell alone. There was a bunk along the side of the wall. It wasn't even big enough to move around in. I don't even remember what we did for a bathroom.

From there, we were sent to Frankfurt, Germany, to a prisoner of war camp. After about two weeks, they shaved all our hair off. That's where we, as prisoners, began to accumulate. We were among the very first twenty-five to thirty prisoners captured over there. We're talking about the very first part of the war in Europe. There was another batch of prisoners captured about the same time at Corregidor.

At our air base in England, we had been in a barracks which was about forty feet square. There were roughly twenty-five of us in there. When a plane got shot down (the one or two that were shot down before we were), they'd come in and take out five or six beds and all the personal belongings. I thought about how we must have been missed after we were shot down, just like the others before us. There were ten on a crew and when they didn't come back, it was pretty rough to miss ten men. Back in those early days if we made three missions and got back home, we were lucky.

New prisoners began to come in. Some days just one, some days six or eight men. We got up to about five hundred. From there they redistributed us to other places. They put us in a box car and shipped us up north and we stayed there for a while. Then we were taken to Munich, Stalag VII A. We were there for about three months. Then the G.I.s were coming in everyday. We got up to about one thousand of us. Then they put us in a box car and shipped us to a place near Poland. We were there for a short time. Then they shipped us again.

There were about eighty men in each box car. No windows. The air could not circulate. The doors had barbed wire in them. There were no sanitary facilities. The only thing they had was one little pot over in the corner. And nobody wanted to get near that pot. It was just awful. We were on the box car for about five days. I don't really remember what we may have had to eat. Maybe some bread, or blood sausage. There would be one can of blood sausage for so many men. Later on we'd have that blood sausage. It was hard to get down. Congealed blood. We'd try to cook it on a little piece of metal with fire underneath. We thought it would fry, but the congealed blood melted. At first, we couldn't eat it. It just wouldn't go down.

So, we were in Stalag III B, then VII A, and after about a week, we ended up in Krems, Austria, near Vienna, which was Stalag XVII B. We accumulated to about three thousand of us. We stayed there longer than any of the other places. It was our last place until the end of the war. Some of the Canadians who'd been at Dunquerque were in the same prison camp as me.

They were bitter against the English. They felt they'd been used as guinea pigs at Dunquerque.

We didn't have to do any work out in the field, or on the railway tracks, or in the mines because of rank as sergeant or higher. This was under the provisions of the Geneva Convention. We just stayed more or less in that one area which had about ten or twelve buildings. There were about three hundred-fifty men in each building. We were all closed in with barbed wire. We'd walk around the compound most of the day. We'd talk to each other. Mostly about eating and home. Talking about eating made it worse, but it was the only thing on our minds. We all ended up with sores all over our bodies from lack of vitamins. We slept a lot. When you're real hungry, all you can do is sleep anyway.

They served us some kind of coffee in the morning. At noon we got a can of soup, if you want to call it soup. It was dehydrated rutabaga. That sure didn't help the diarrhea. Sometimes we'd get barley soup. At night, we'd get maybe one potato, a small one. There'd be one loaf of bread for eight men. The person who would cut the bread was responsible for breaking it off into equal pieces. He would be the last one to choose his piece, so he'd get the one left over. This helped keep everyone halfway honest. This was during the last six months of the war. It wasn't like this in the beginning. It was worse in the beginning when we didn't get anything.

The Germans were broadcasting news over to the United States. And somebody along the line would hear the names and serial numbers of prisoners of war being held by the Germans. The people who heard would let families know their sons were alive. That was the way my parents first heard news of me after I'd been missing for a while. I got to write home a few times, but had to be careful what I wrote otherwise the Germans wouldn't send it through. These were on post cards.

And then the Russians were coming in. We could hear their guns off in the distance. I've often wondered why they made us march from Stalag XVII B in Krems to Munich. We walked in the Alps through frozen mountains. We spent more than thirty days marching from Vienna to Munich. We marched on the roads. We wore shoes they issued to us, wooden-style sandal type shoes. We got blisters and everything else. It was the first part of April and it was very cold. In the nighttime we stayed in the woods. Once or twice we were able to get into a barn to sleep at night. It was cold, with rain and sleet. I don't remember having any soup to eat. I remember eating wild greens from the side of the road, like onions. We'd just pull up a little piece and eat it. They must have given us something to eat, but I don't remember.

One time they took us to a stream. We were all filthy and dirty. We all washed up in that stream. You can imagine three thousand G.I.s trying to wash up in a little stream.

It was getting close to the end of the war then and I can remember the Americans would fly over us. I get emotional at the memory...The planes would tip their wings to let us know who they were and that they knew we were down there. We knew they wouldn't bomb us. The wing tipping let us know they were friendly planes. We were always fearful of being bombed, especially when they had us on those box cars.

Because they had us marching all the time, we were exhausted and worn out, and we were sick with dysentery. Sometimes one of us would just fall off the side of the road. Under those conditions, dysentery will kill a man in a minute. Instead of the Germans trying to nurse him back to health, they'd just shoot him and get rid of him if he couldn't keep up. This was particularly the way they treated the Russian people and the Jewish people. But it was the Russians they treated the worst, the worse by far, worse than anybody else.

We were out in the woods, east of Munich near Salzburg, about a week. We learned how to make little huts. We'd put the pine limbs on top. The water would come in eventually, but most of the water would just run off that roof. We had a long latrine out there. I remember where they put long logs for the fellows to sit on. One time the log gave way and all the fellows fell into the latrine. Of course, we all had diarrhea and dysentery.

If a German was captured by a Russian, he would kill himself so that he would not be sent to the Siberian front. The Germans did not want to go there. That scared the hell out of them. The Americans told the Germans if they didn't treat them better, the Russians were going to come in and take them to Siberia. This was when the war was nearly over.

Because we'd been able to get little two-way radios, we knew the war was almost over. When we got parcels, which might contain a D-Bar of candy, we could give that candy to a German guard. That German guard would supply us with a crystal. Then another might sneak in a piece of wire. Then we'd put that wire on top of the crystal. Someone else would get in the headphones, which would cost a big price, like a pack of cigarettes or a D-

Bar ration. These were items we might receive in a Red Cross parcel. There might be oleo, corned beef, or salmon in there. You'd be fascinated with what the G.I.s connived. With a D-Bar of candy we could trade with the Germans, maybe slip in a chicken, which was only once in a great long while. It wasn't exactly like "Hogan's Heroes!"

We were there in the camp near Munich, and then we could hear the Americans coming off in the distance. We could hear the artillery, the shelling. It took two or three days for them to come to where we were. It was General Patton's army that liberated us.

After that we were all given a lot of white pills. This was for the tremendous cases of diarrhea and dysentery. After about three days, they began flying us over to the hospital at Le Havre, France. We were there about ten days. Then they put us on a boat and sent us back home. This was about the end of May or first of June, 1945.

Have you ever seen a bunch of folks cry? You can imagine all us having been "tied up" like that for so long. It had been roughly three years since I left home. When we first got back to the United States, we landed in New York City. I can remember seeing the Statue of Liberty. As we were getting off the ship, the three thousand of us could hear the tune "Don't Fence Me In" playing over the loud speakers. We thought it was dedicated to us only. We were in our glory walking off that ship onto the land.

I ended up in Hattiesburg, Mississippi, at Camp Shelby. When my folks came to get me, I didn't recognize them. My younger brother had grown up. They were more or less strangers to me in a way. But I was so happy; I was in orbit. I remember the first can of beer I drank when I got to Camp Shelby. I don't remember where I got it from. Maybe the Red Cross gave it to me. That one can of beer got me so drunk from not drinking anything at all for a long time.

One of the fellows in our camp from California, Ben Phelper, kept a diary and kept it hidden from the Germans. He managed to get a camera and film and took pictures of our camp, Stalag XVII B. When he got back from the war, he had a book published with all the pictures. He had handwritten the whole book: a firsthand account of our time spent there. You can imagine he must have made a fortune from this. As we liked to say, "We were guests in Stalag XVII B." A person has to keep a sense of humor.

Philip T. Cascio

Many, many years after the war, around 1980, my wife and I traveled to Europe. We went to Munich, Germany. There was a big party given for us and the group we were with. It was at Lowenbrau Brewery. A German man who was the hotel manager at the Hilton Hotel where we were staying was there. He was a great big fellow. He was sharply dressed and carried a walking cane, like the big kind a shepherd would carry. We began talking about the war. The conversation was friendly. He recognized me and said to me, "I could have killed you because I was a guard at your camp." I didn't really recognize him. But we both became emotional and started crying. We two became big celebrities that night. Our names were announced over the loud speaker and they played music especially for us. I believe I remember that they played "Don't Fence Me In."

There have been lots of good things about my life; but there are lots of things I would change. One thing, I would get some education. When I came back, I thought I knew all the answers. Nobody could tell me anything at all. I didn't want to go back to school. I lacked only about nine hours in my pre-law degree, but I thought I knew everything and didn't want to go back anymore. I got lucky when I got into business and became successful. Now I want to be remembered as just a good old fellow.

Before I went to the war, I did not have a sense of patriotism; and I didn't have any when I was in the war. For years, it was a dead issue. It came on as I got older and began to think about things like that. Don't take anything you've got for granted. That sums it up.

Chapter Seven

Raoul Jacques De Lier

October 6, 1998

I was born of French-Canadian descent in Minot, North Dakota, in 1919. My paternal grandfather was a civil engineer and city planner back in the old railroad days. My maternal grandfather came from Ireland in the late 1800s and worked building the railroad. It was due to the railroad that my mother and father met and married.

I took ROTC in college and was in the horsedrawn field artillery, which I didn't like much. I went with a friend of mine to enlist in the naval air corps. There was a long line there, but right across the hall was the army air corps with no line. So we went over there and that's how I got in the United States Army Air Corps. I was a navigator in the Ninth Air Force, 394th Bombardment Group, 586th Squadron. We were fighters and medium bombardment, twin engine bombers- the tactical air force.

I had a lot of experience before the war. I was in flying school before World War II started, and I had graduated from college. My first duty station out of flying school in August 1941 was at Barksdale Air Force Base in Shreveport, Louisiana. I was the squadron navigation officer and instructor of a group which was training pilots and crews to go overseas. I was there for almost eighteen months. In fact, I thought I would spend the whole war there. But when I went into the office one day to ask for a leave, I was told I was leaving all right, but not to go home to see my family. I would be going to Battle Creek, Michigan, to join a combat group which was getting ready to go overseas. That's where I joined the 394th Bombardment Group in October 1943, and we left for overseas in February 1944. I was twenty-five years old when I went over to Europe.

When I left for Europe, I didn't have much fear. We flew from West Palm Beach, Florida, to Puerto Rico where we loaded up with all the booze we could put on the airplane; then to British Guyana where the air strip was hewn right out of the jungle, and we slept in thatched huts which were up on stilts to keep the water out; then we flew across the Brazilian Rain Forest to Belem at the mouth of the Amazon River; then to Natal, Brazil, for about three days; and then to Ascension Island, a little spot in the ocean about halfway from South America to Africa. Our next stop was in Liberia where a funny thing happened. Again, we were in thatched huts on the bank of a river. Some people were coming across the river in dugout canoes. They were real natives, complete with loin clothes. They had Four Seasons liquor for sale which they'd stolen off previous planes!

From Liberia, we flew to Dakar in French Equatorial Africa; then across Spanish Sahara to Marrakech, Morocco, where we spent twenty days waiting on favorable winds. Then, finally, from Marrakech we flew our longest flight all over water to Land's End, England. We couldn't risk head winds because we would barely have enough gas under the best conditions. We were briefed every morning about four o'clock. If the meteorological report was not favorable, then we were free the rest of the day in Marrakech. There was a beautiful old hotel there which was world famous. It was called La Mamounia Hotel, and it's where Winston Churchill kept his headquarters during the war. We would go in there and hang around, have a drink or two. It was in the casbah or native section of Marrakech which was an experience in itself. We saw veiled women on the street who thought nothing of urinating or defecating in public on the hard-packed dirt streets.

From Land's End, we went to our base at Boreham which was near Chelmsford, England. A couple of months before D-Day we were moved to Holmsley South near Bournemouth right off the Isle of Wight. From there we flew to France.

We went into Normandy on July 13, 1944. We were operating off landing strips near Saint Mere-Eglise, France. Our landing strip was hewn from an apple orchard. This was in the area of the Calvados producers. We were living there in tents until August. We bathed and shaved out of our helmets to clean up. We soaked our dirty old clothes, our woolen uniforms, in aviation fuel. We dug a slit trench for a latrine out in the back about eighty yards from the tents. The Germans had already been in this area for quite a few years. Some of the German soldiers had married French girls and had families around there where we were. And some of them didn't retreat from the area after D-Day. They stayed around there and wore civilian clothes. Sometimes during the night when our men would get up to use the slit trench, these Germans would attack them and cut their throats. It happened two or three times. The group commander issued an order that any man having to out there after dark had to take a companion with him. You can imagine that you're tired and sleepy, and somebody wakes you up and says, "I've got to go." So, you have to get up and take your gun and go with him and stay there while he does his duty. Fortunately, that lasted only a week until all the leftover Germans were ferreted out.

Then we went to Orleans, France, which was the home of Saint Joan of Arc. From there we went to the Belgium border near Cambrai, France. At Orleans and Cambrai we were on captured German airfields. We bombed V-1 missile sites, troop replacements, marshalling yards, bridges, and ammunition dumps. At Cambrai I flew my sixty-eighth mission and was sent home.

Our plane was the B-26, the Martin Marauder. There were six to ten men on each crew. The larger crews had a G-Box radar and they occupied the lead planes. These crews had the extra men: navigator, bombardier, flight control officer, and gunner control officer. The lead plane had the bomb sight on it and when the lead plane dropped its bombs, then the rest of the planes toggled theirs. We flew in echelons of three, flights of six, and boxes of eighteen. The lead plane in each flight of six had the Norden bomb sight in it. When you took off for the target, you flew to what was called the I.P. or initial point. Then you'd make a turn, and from then on, the lead bombardier flew your airplane. You couldn't take any evasive action. He had the Norden bomb sight connected to the controls and guided you from that instrumentation. So, from the I.P., which was usually about fifteen miles from the target, you were a sitting duck. You just had to sit there. You couldn't take any evasive action. In the early days of the Normandy Invasion, we got shot at a lot from the ground by our own side when we flew along the front lines. Later, we learned to make a U-turn and avoid those front lines.

On a mission to bomb Caen, France, we got hit badly and I became injured by flak from antiaircraft fire. I was hit in the face and in my rear. The bombardier was wounded worse than me. The waist gunner and tail gunner were killed. One of the wire mesh cables was hit and it splintered into thousands of pieces. This was what hit my face. For ten years afterward, I would get pieces of steel out of my face when shaving. As we approached for landing back in England, we fired a red flare to indicate we had wounded aboard. This signaled them to have the ambulances out. When we attempted to land, the wheels wouldn't go down, so we had to land on our belly. That was quite an experience, too. Here we had dead guys on board, and two injured, and we were thinking, "Oh, my God, we got back this far, and now the engines are going to catch fire on landing and blow up the plane." But it didn't.

War is hell. We didn't have it like the infantry or artillery where you're out slogging around. We normally had enough food and a warm place to sleep. At one time we were moving so fast up behind the troops that our supply lines didn't catch up with us. We were being fed by the First Army. We got what they didn't want. For three days we had coffee and orange marmalade. That's all we had. And I can't look orange marmalade in the face to this day!

I went over there and did what they told me to do, and came home. That was about the extent of my story. We lost a lot of people. I saw planes blown up along side ours and I lost friends almost everyday. That was tough. But it wasn't as bad as fighting on the ground. Each mission was much like the other. You got up, and you took off, and you got shot at, and you dropped your bombs. And if you were lucky, you got back.

There was a points system which included the number of years you served on active duty and the number of decorations you had, which added up to points. You got so much for each year, each wound, and each medal. When I got back I was stationed as an instructor at San Marcos, Texas. I was home on leave when VE-Day was declared which was in May 1945. I went back and checked in at eight o'clock in the morning. They said if I could get checked out by seven o'clock that night that I was out of there. One other man and I had the highest points on the base. It took me about three minutes to make up my mind. By that night I was on the road going back to Oklahoma City.

I was alive and well and young. People who were working at that time were either old men or younger guys who weren't in the service. The war was just over in Europe and those men weren't back yet. Prior to World War II, I worked for MGM and RKO as a clerk during the summer months, so I had some experience in the motion picture industry. There was a job opening at Universal Pictures and they hired me. The first day I went to work for them, they took me to New York. In the motion picture business there were three areas: distribution or sales, exhibition or theaters, and production or movie-making. I was in the distribution end of the business. So, I started out selling motion pictures. I was transferred all over the country and grew tired of that. One of my accounts was Video Theaters which owned about five hundred theaters in Oklahoma, Texas, Arizona, and southern California. They were one of the purchasers of television station KWTV Channel 9 in Oklahoma City and responsible for putting it on the air. They signed on the air in December 1953. The president of Video Theaters asked me if I wanted to come to work for them. I told him I didn't know anything about television. He said, "Well, neither does anyone else." I went to work for them on January 8, 1954, as the national sales manager. Then I became the station manager, and eventually the president and general manager. I was there for twenty-eight years. I retired in 1982.

My age group of people went through school during The Depression. Very few people had much then. There wasn't any peer pressure as far as material possessions.

As a child, I went to Catholic grade school. The nuns were very tough. Discipline was bred into me. Then I went to a Jesuit prep school, the Creighton Preparatory School in Omaha, Nebraska. The Jesuits were great teachers, great philosophers. But they were also pretty tough. I had four years of Latin and three years of Greek. It made my mind function. I can still remember the opening line of "Virgil."

My former football coach at Creighton Prep was instrumental in my attending the University of Oklahoma. I got into the discipline of college athletics immediately. Unfortunately for me, my athletic career was shortened by a severe leg injury.

Even my home life had been disciplined. If my dad told me to be home at midnight, I was home at midnight. It wasn't because I was afraid he would beat me up or anything like that. I just didn't want to worry him.

So, I was prepared for military service. It wasn't anything that bothered me. I'm still that way. If someone of authority tells me to jump, I ask which way and how far. I don't say I don't like that. I do what I'm told to do, although I may think something different. I think that's indicative of most people my age. It seems like members of the younger generation think whatever they want to do is right and to hell with anybody else.

My life seemed to line me up to be a leader. I was president of the student council in high school, captain of the baseball team in high school, and president of our college fraternity. Later I was president of the Better Business Bureau, president of the Oklahoma Telecasters Association, president of the Oklahoma City Golf and Country Club twice, president of the Air and Space Museum, president of the Waterford Association, president of the Waterford Home Owners Association, and trustee of Saint Gregory's College. I guess some way or another I gravitated toward a position of leadership. Other people have put responsibility on me and I've taken it. I've had a pretty interesting life.

I want to be remembered for honesty and integrity. In my era of business, a handshake was sufficient. Your word was your bond. This is why it's so difficult for people my age to see politics and chicanery going on the way it is today. John L. Lewis was president of the Congress of Industrial Organizations in 1938. When he got mad at President Franklin D. Roosevelt and the unions, he said, "A pox on both your houses." That's the way I feel about this President Clinton issue and the ridiculousness of both the Democrats and the Republicans.

One thing I would change about my life if I could is that my wife and I would have liked to have had more children if possible. Also, I would have been kinder to people when I was in a position of authority. I wasn't always kind, but I thought I was always fair. My fairness was sometimes overridden by being picayunish and dogmatic. I didn't always handle all affairs with great aplomb. I wouldn't change much, but I would have studied harder. I didn't realize the opportunity I had while I was in school. In my age group, not one out of ten got the opportunity to go to college. I wasn't as determined as I should have been to get a good education. I wasted my time a lot and I shouldn't have. I could have been more prepared by studying harder.

Going directly into the service from college helped me. I was prepared to go to work, and to work hard when I got out. I was much more mature when I got out of the service. I didn't have goals as such, but I realized what I had

Raoul Jacques De Lier

to do to accomplish something. I knew that if I wanted to be successful I had to apply myself, and I didn't have that feeling prior to the military service.

The four years I spent in the Jesuit prep school at Creighton influenced my life more than anything. It wasn't anyone in particular, but the Jesuit order as a whole. My experience there still influences my life. But my wife has had the greatest influence on my life. I met her at a fraternity Christmas dance in 1937. I never had another date in my life after I met her. We've been together sixty years. And it's been sixty years of pleasure, beyond anything I can think of.

I've lived each day as it came along. I haven't tried to conform to any particular adage. Being a Catholic has been the most motivating factor in my life. A favorite verse of mine from the Book of 2 Timothy is: "I have fought the good fight, I have finished the race, I have kept the faith."

CHAPTER EIGHT

EARNEST C. FREEMAN

JULY 29,1998

I was in the Thirteenth Air Force, Fifth Bomb Group, Seventy-second Squadron in the South Pacific. We flew B-24s. I flew two tours: one in the North Pacific and one in the South Pacific.

I graduated from high school in 1940 and went to college with the idea of playing basketball. In the fall of 1940, I got into the National Guard because they paid a dollar a drill. Boy, I needed that dollar bad because I didn't have anything. Just after I got in the National Guard, they mobilized it in 1941. We were told it would be for only one year, then they'd let us out to come back to college. They started the draft about that time, but I wasn't old enough for the draft, so I didn't even have to register.

I was sent to El Paso, Texas. When the war started, I was in Tacoma, Washington. Then I was sent up to Seattle where the Boeing Aircraft Factory was. I was in an antiaircraft outfit at that time. About eighteen days after the war started, I was sent to the Aleutian Islands, Dutch Harbor. I was there when the Japanese bombed it on June 3, 1942. That was a hellhole. Then the war was about six months old. It was at about the same time that Midway was bombed by the Japanese. After Dutch Harbor, I was sent back to the States.

I went through a cadet program when I was twenty-one years old. Our time off from cadet school was from noon Saturday until noon Sunday. We had to be back in time for the parade that was held every Sunday. There'd be

20,000 people there. It was a huge parade that lasted almost four hours. They had marching bands that would give me chills. I graduated from cadet school in December 1943, then went to flight school and came out a bombardier. Next, I was in combat phase training. That's where I picked up the whole crew and we had training as a crew. I was made a flight instructor.

It was at this time I met Phyllis and we decided to get married. As soon as I got back from getting married, I got my orders to ship out. It was the very next morning I had to leave. But when I got where I was going, I was told there would be a delay. So, Phyllis took a train and met me in Harrington, Kansas. We became friends with Charles Brown and his wife. Like us, they had just gotten married. Charles was a navigator and a Harvard graduate. We found out that Charles and I were being sent to San Francisco, California, on the train with first class tickets. Charles asked if they would give us the money instead and let us buy four coach tickets so our wives could go with us. They did.

When we got to San Francisco, we put our wives in a hotel. The hotel required seeing our marriage licenses before they'd let us have a room! And there was a five-day limit at the hotel because San Francisco was overrun with service people.

Charles and I went on out to the base. After about three or four days, we found out that we two were replacing a bombardier and navigator who had been killed in a crash. The pilot of that crew had gone off his rocker, we were told. They thought this crew needed some time off, so we were given a furlough.

Phyllis and I came back to my parents' home in Arkansas. We were there about ten days before I had to leave to return to San Francisco. From there, I went on to Hawaii and was there two weeks. Then I went to Guadalcanal where we started flying out. I flew forty-four missions. I never went down and I never had to bail out, but we got shot up a lot. We got shot up the first mission I flew on.

That first mission I went on, I got a rude awakening. They told me all the things to expect from combat, but it was beyond my comprehension. As the bombardier, I had to learn to do everything without ever thinking, because once we were in combat I couldn't think about which switches to turn and what intervals to set. When we were in combat, I was thinking about getting hit. We had fighters jumping us before we ever got to the target. The first time I flew over a target, some huge shells came up and burst. They made big black spots and I knew those had missed us. By then, the fighters were out of the way because they didn't want to risk getting hit by the shells. Our tail gunner got hit. It injured the whole back of his head. He was out like a light. I'd had some first aid courses. All I could remember was being told, "Sulfanilamide- you can't use too much of it!" So, one of the other gunners and I piled on the sulfanilamide and put gauze all over it. By the time we got through with him, he looked like a mummy! But he lived. Pretty soon, he was flying again. He crashed on take-off one day and survived. Then they sent him home. They said he was too snake-bit.

That first mission really broke me in good. I don't think anybody else was as scared as I was.

Later, I was flying with the same crew, and our nose turret gunner got shot up by fighter fire. He was right there close to me when he got hit. We got him out of that turret and gave him first aid. He lived, too. But he never flew anymore.

We had four guys to each tent. The Japanese would bomb us every night, and we'd bomb them during the day. They'd keep us up half the night. I only had to fly about every third day. A fellow named Hodges, who was the navigator on my original crew, was with us in our tent. He was grounded because he'd been hurt on a crash, and then got shot down on his next mission a month later. He was waiting to go home, back to Amarillo, Texas. It was almost five months he stayed with us before he got to go. We were under really heavy bombing at night. They were big bombs. And we could hear the flak falling through the trees. One morning, the rest of us went on a mission, and when we got back, Hodges had us the best foxhole you've ever seen in your life. He'd dug it so deep, you could almost walk in it. He'd put benches in it, and a sand bag, and had covered the top with planks made from the coconut trees. He'd done everything!

We had a little old dog we called "Rebel" because he was said to have been bought in South Australia. He was the only dog on Morotai Island, just south of the Philippines. Three shots from an antiaircraft gun was the signal which indicated we were going to have an air raid. Then a single shot signaled all clear. Rebel was so smart and had learned from hearing these signals so often, that when he heard the three shots, he would beat us to the foxhole! Old Rebel would be sitting there waiting on us when we got there.

* * *

I had a good friend named Founce. He was an old country boy from Iowa, and I was another old country boy from Arkansas. So we kind of hit it off because we had the same upbringing. His bombardier was sick one time, and Founce asked if I could fly with him the next day. So, I said, “Sure, I’ll fly with you.” And Founce said he’d ask operations to let me fly with him. When we went down for the briefing, we found they’d called a shipping strike. A shipping strike meant waiting until those ships got within your range before they let you leave. These were destroyers and aircraft carriers, and we didn’t like those because they were pretty dangerous. Then I wished I hadn’t agreed to go with Founce. The next day we went down to the flight line where we waited and waited. A bunch of the guys were sitting around under the wings playing cards waiting for their name call. By about three o’clock in the afternoon, we were told it was too late to do anything and to go back to camp. The next day we went through the same thing. Whenever it got close to dark, we had to cancel the mission because we couldn’t see. This was before radar, and our targets were five to six hours away. The next day, the ships still weren’t in our range, so we couldn’t do anything. By the next day, the crew’s original bombardier was well, so I didn’t have to replace him. He went with the crew when they finally took off. They didn’t come back.

Eventually, all the officers on my crew got killed but me. They were substituting for other crews when they got killed. I was the only one of my crew who came out of it. My old friend Charles Brown was killed, too. He bailed out and was never found. The Japs were bad about strafing the parachuters after they bailed. Maybe that’s what happened to him. I was on a mission that same day and knew we lost some planes, but I didn’t know it was his. Everyone on his crew was recovered but him. He and his wife had a child born on my birthday. He never got to see that child.

I flew two missions which each went for sixteen and one-half hours in the air. That was the longest a B-24 had ever stayed in the air. These missions were to bomb the oil fields where the Japanese were getting all their fuel. It took four days to bomb out one of them. We began getting less fighters on us as they began to run out of fuel. I finished my missions the day before Christmas 1944. It was hard getting a way home because the planes headed in that direction had priority for the wounded. There was no room for us. We got home on a passenger ship loaded with troops. We had to sleep out on the deck, and it took twenty-six days to reach San Francisco. I got home in the spring of 1945 before the war in Europe was over.

I began training as a navigator. The new plan was to make the bombardier and navigator the same man. I was about to go back again. I didn't know what I was going to have to do, but I knew they weren't going to let me stay in the States. Meanwhile, the war over in Europe ended. And then Japan was bombed before I had to go back.

* * *

We had patriotism back then. It meant each person had to do his part. There were people who wanted to serve and were turned down. There was a man who had only one hand. He wanted to get it in, but they wouldn't take him. He had a good mind, and he would have been a good supply man. Patriotism now is just not the same. Now people try to keep from having to go. Back then, I would have never tried to get out of going into the army. I felt like I was supposed to be doing this. It was my duty. The feeling of patriotism is like what I would get at those parades each Sunday at cadet school. It was a tingle; a proud feeling. I wanted to do everything I could for my country. And there were the people who were good to those who were in the service. They'd cash our checks from back home and help us out in many ways. That was another kind of patriotism.

I've thought a lot about the boys who got killed, and didn't have the chance to get old like I have. They wouldn't believe the way things are now, and some of the things we go through. And this is what they got themselves killed for- would they think it was worth it?

A man going out on a mission didn't think he was the one who was going to get killed that day. He thought it would be somebody else. He knew some planes would be lost, but he knew, or thought, it wouldn't be his. After flying a mission and coming back, it was like a victory. Everyone was cheerful, exhilarated from the win. We'd get in the tent and laugh and have fun and talk about funny things that had happened that day. It was a celebration. That's how we got by.

Earnest C. Freeman

One time we'd gotten back from a mission, and we were all in the tent. We were laughing and whooping it up, really having a good time. One of the boys was sitting over there, real quiet. We asked him why. He said he thought he must be different from us because the bombing missions scared him to death. He said, "I pray. And you may laugh at me, but I pray." Nobody laughed at him. They were doing the same thing... praying.

And there was someone who prayed a lot for me while I was in the war. It was my mother-in-law. You just had to know her. She was a good woman, a religious woman. She loved history, and she kept up with everything going on in the world. Although she did not talk about it, you could ask her and she would know what was going on. She influenced me and my life. She never said a bad word about anybody. Material things didn't matter to her, and she never complained about anything. She was a person to look up to. I respected her so much I couldn't even drink a beer in front of her. She was a hero to me.

I've thought about it a lot, and I wouldn't change anything about my life. It all turned out good. The only regret I have is that I didn't go on and finish college. I came back and went into the furniture business and it turned out just as well. I'm proud we were able to educate our children. No, I wouldn't change anything, because if I did I might not have met my wife, or have my six grandchildren.

I've often said my goal in life was to be the oldest living bombardier in the United States! But, mainly, I want to be remembered as a family man, one whose grandson wants to come play golf with his seventy-six-year-old granddad. And mine does.

Chapter Nine

William Warren Gooch

July 29, 1998

My mother had to sign for me to join the military. I was only seventeen years old. Then they put the draft on for my age group. That was in 1942. I was in the Desert Air Force, stationed in Libya… the Americans and the Free French. We didn't have much of anything. I think we only had three planes. That was the very beginning of it.

I trained on B-17 planes, but ended up on B-24s. I was a sergeant, a waist-gunner. Then, after reorganization, I was in the Ninth Air Force, Ninety-eighth Bomb Group, 344th Squadron. Colonel John R. Kane was our group commander. He was also a surgeon. He's the most brave man I ever saw because he wouldn't let us go anywhere he wouldn't go. We'd get back and he would go work all night with the injured. If his mission was called off and he wasn't going, he wouldn't let us go. He was different. He cared about his men.

I had several crashes. When they flew us out of Germany, after we were liberated, it was in an old stripped-down B-17, which had to belly-land because the landing gear wouldn't come down. There were about one hundred men on that plane. That was my fifth time. On other occasions, I bailed out twice; flew into the ground once and walked off; and flew into the water once, the Mediterranean, and only two of us got out. God was looking out after us, I guess. But we weren't thinking about things like that. That's why they had to have young people to be good soldiers. You need people who will take chances and get things done. We were taught at one time not to get too familiar with our crew, but you had to look out for your buddies

I flew on a mission to a Rumanian oil field which was at Ploiesti on August 1, 1943. It was a big raid. There were a lot of planes from England and everywhere else. We were in the air thirteen hours and fifty-five minutes. We couldn't get back; we crash landed on Malta. We'd left Benghazi, Libya, early before daylight. We flew across at fifty feet altitude. We flew low so radar couldn't pick us up. We flew so low that there were corn stalks and grass caught in the bottom of the planes. It was a secret thing. We were in the second wave and had delayed bombs. Our lead group got lost. It took them about forty-five minutes to get back on track. They were first in and went in and dropped their bombs. Then when we got there on schedule, the lead group's bombs were just going off. Everything was in disarray. There was smoke; debris flying everywhere. Airplanes were going everywhere, being blown up. I don't know how in the world we ever got out. It was our own stuff blowing us up. I saw only one or two German fighter planes, but they weren't any threat. Even so, the mission did not look like a failure to me, because it looked like the whole world was being blown up down there.

After limping on to Malta, we stayed four days, and came on back to Benghazi. We had about one hundred-eighty holes in our plane. Some of them you could crawl through, and nobody got a scratch. It was miraculous. We had to leave the plane there. We couldn't even get it off the ground.

The German general, Rommel, was over in the desert. The British beat him out of the desert and went on to Sicily. Then they invaded Italy, and that's the day I got shot down. It was September 3, 1943. It was about my seventeenth mission. We were going to bomb a rail yard southeast of Rome. When we got there, they were just waiting for us. It was the first time I had encountered any fighter planes that amounted to anything, but they came at us from everywhere. They shot down almost all of us. I heard later that only one plane out of our squadron of twelve got back. On that day I got shot down, there was a boy with us. He'd already flown his last mission. He was a co-pilot and just went along for the ride. We had eleven aboard that day. We were over the Adriatic Sea when they jumped us. That boy didn't make it. His parachute didn't open. I just barely made it in to land. I bailed out and hit the tail of the plane (B-24). It snapped my head back. There was a big knot on my forehead for a long time. I broke my neck and my leg.

The tail gunner was the last to bail. I saw him get out, but I never saw him again until we found ourselves in the same civilian jail. This jail was a prison built into rock and was three or four stories high. The Italians half carried me in - first through a cellar door, then a long tunnel, and through several iron gates. I was on the highest level. I was a prisoner until the end of the war. I never again saw any of the rest of my crew after we were shot down.

Then the Italians put me on a farm for about six weeks. I was with some Australian prisoners. We never got any of the vegetables from the fields we were working. They'd search us to make sure. They would nudge us along with rifle butts, hitting us in the kidneys. I stayed sore all the time.

It was a year before my parents knew what had happened to me. After a year, you were declared dead. But right at the eleventh month, they gave us something to write a message to our parents to tell them where we were and that we were okay, you had to say you were okay. They said they were going to broadcast it over the radio, and they did. Someone told my mother about it, and then my parents got a letter from the American Red Cross telling them that I was alive.

I was in Italy from September 1943 until late November 1943. Then the Italians essentially gave up when the British invaded them. The Germans moved me to a camp near Rome. The Germans spent more of their time taking the Italian soldiers and civilians to Germany for slave labor. Then I was moved again. It took us thirteen days on the train to get from just below Rome to Frankfurt. There were many delays because the tracks had been bombed. I tell you, I was in tough shape in Italy. The dang train trips were tough as they moved us around. They'd put all those they could get into a box car. Cold or hot weather. Of course, when it was cold, the more they put in there, the warmer we'd stay. There weren't any sanitary facilities; some of the men would get sick. The drinking water they would bring us on the train was usually from ditches. That gave some of the men dysentery. It was a hell of a mess. But it never made me sick. How, I don't know.

I was in solitary confinement in Frankfurt for fifty-seven days, with a broken leg and a broken neck. It was in a little old bitty place, a rat hole, dirty. The Germans said they were trying to find out whether my parents had left Germany prior to 1939, because of my last name. I was finally cleared.

They didn't feed us. We were dirty- didn't have baths or anything. I've gone two or three times six months without a bath, and that's pretty horrible. We had infestations of lice; bedbugs; sand fleas. They would just eat you up.

I wasn't that tough when I went in. But I could always do almost anything I wanted to. I never thought about giving up. Sometimes I may have dreamed about giving up, but eventually I'd come back to reality. I knew I had to survive. I knew it would be over some day.

I was in Stalag XVII B in Vienna, Austria, for about two weeks. The Germans harassed us all the time. They said we knew too much. If you were sitting down, they wanted you to stand up; if you were asleep, get up. They never let you rest. I guess they wanted to wear us out and see what they could find out. They asked about our units. They probably knew more than we did about it.

Next, we were sent to a camp near Munich. I got with another group of about forty-seven RAF boys. I stayed with them all during the war. I was the only American in the bunch. We were all sick then. Several hundred of us. I stayed sick all winter long. I almost died. Mainly the way we passed our time was to sleep. We really didn't think about anything unless there was a book to read. An Australian who was in the camp with me was a college graduate engineer. His father owned a shipping company. He taught me math. That was beneficial to me and it took up a lot of time. He began teaching me like I didn't know anything. And I didn't! Some of the other men with me were Ezra Pound, the controversial American author and poet who was living in Italy, a Spanish prince, an English school teacher, and a Choctaw Indian chief who died of tuberculosis in the upper bunk. I came to know Ezra Pound pretty well. He was very intelligent. Really just a regular old guy. We became pretty good friends. I learned later of his espionage. He'd been picked up trying to get across the mountains into Spain. The others were members of the RAF who were sons of the English aristocracy. They were smart! They could take nothing and make something from it to survive. I was the only Yankee there. I was fortunate to be with the English RAF boys because they had been there a long time and they knew the Germans just like you'd know your neighbors.

I don't know where the days went. I remember it was cold a lot. I barely remember the summer time. I guess because it was nice. Our clothes were always the same. Wool.

I just remember the winters, gosh, snow and ice. Barley stew was one of the foods we were given to eat. Now and then it would have a little meat in it, some potatoes and carrots. We had black bread which had to be divided among ourselves, so many men per loaf. It was very heavy, and the crust on it was so hard you couldn't bite it. You had to soak it in something, usually water. We had water most of the time.

I spent the winter of 1944 in Lithuania, near the border of Finland. It was cold as all get-out, sixty degrees below zero. You couldn't go outside or you'd freeze to death. I got sick that winter. It was terrible.

Then they brought us down away from the Russians to another camp. Then up to what we called Luft Three. That was the first time I was ever permanently assigned to an American camp. And it was for American flyers. By then, the war was over. By then, I weighed only eighty-two pounds. I was a prisoner for more than eighteen months.

It really didn't hit me I was going home until I got back to the United States. I went to France first and stayed there about a month. The camp we went to in Le Harve, France, was called Lucky Strike. There were people from everywhere. All denominations. All the POWs and those coming in for repatriation. Some were coming out of hospitals and on their way home. They had a mess hall we called "transit." You could go eat there anytime you wanted to. But we couldn't eat much. The first night, several of us died, just from overeating. Too much shock. We had to just eat a little bit at a time until our stomachs were back in order. Then I came home on a troop ship. They just dumped us off and gave us a ticket and some money and told us to go home. It was then that I realized that I was really free. It took me a while to get used to it. I didn't want to say much about it. I just wanted to get myself together and gain a little weight. I'd lost over fifty pounds during my imprisonment.

It was October or November 1944 when I was discharged and finally came back to my hometown. That was during game season. I liked to hunt, so I just took to the woods. I'd get up every morning and go to the woods. Rain or shine. I'd stay all day. I had an old horse I'd ride down there. I'd tie him to the fence and take off into the woods. After I was home for a month, I went to Miami Beach, Florida where they had a re-pat thing for us. Repatriation. It was to help us get back to our senses. I was there for three months.

I think people have lost all reality of what war is about. You just have to be there to know about it. I never talked too much about my experience to my family. Over the years I might say a thing or two, then they finally put it all together. I just didn't want to talk about it.

When I first got back, I couldn't get any medical treatment. Or money. It took me fifty years to get all my records straightened out. When the Viet Nam boys got back and became lawyers and doctors and senators, they got a bill passed with President Reagan signing it, which gave ex-POWs protocol. That was the first relief we got.

Many years after the war, I went to England. While I was in London, I saw some young German people. It upset me so badly. It was the first time I'd been around any Germans since the war. And I almost flipped at that, but I didn't.

I was very patriotic when I went to war. There wasn't any doubt if we would win. We knew we would, but I didn't know if I was going to get through it. When we were flying, before I was captured, it was just like a job. If we made it back, okay; if we didn't, then that's just what it wound up to be.

When the war started, our country was just coming out of The Depression. No one really had any advantages. Many folks were rural. You know, war is not all bad. A lot of technology comes out of it, new ways to do things. And now there are more than three times as many people as when I was young. I wouldn't change anything, but I sure as heck wouldn't want to go back. I hope no one else has to go back and fight a war, but I know they will. That's just the way it is.

Ours is the best country in the world, regardless of what we don't like. At least we can holler about what we don't like. Everyone getting together is what patriotism is all about. Everyone likes to be free. There's nothing like it. If you ever get to where you can't be free, then you realize what it is. Losing your freedom is like forever being in jail. When I was a prisoner, I promised myself that I'd never do anything to get myself behind another wire fence. I didn't want that again, no matter what it took. I learned to turn my back on things. If somebody doesn't see things the same way I do, then

William Warren Gooch

that's their business, not mine. That's their problem, and I don't worry about it. All of us are heroes in a sense. It takes everybody to do something big. You can't do it by yourself.

I don't care what anyone else says, ours is still the best nation in the world.

Chapter Ten

Fred Henry Gordon, Sr.

November 17, 1998

I was working on the Pickens Farm in Arkansas in 1942 when I had to register for the draft. Back then we only had two tractors on the farm. A really good tractor driver could be kept out of the war for three months or longer. When I was eighteen years old in September, I was classified by the draft as 1-A, which made me priority material. The next thing I knew, in November, I got what they called a "greeting from Uncle Sam" telling me I was accepted in the United States Army. I wasn't afraid about going. It was an education for me.

I was sent to Camp Robinson in Little Rock, Arkansas. I was there from November 15, 1942, until January 22, 1943. I left there on a train for Camp Claiborne in Alexandria, Louisiana. I was there until the month of May when they let me go home for a fifteen-day furlough. Then I was shipped to New York to get ready to go overseas. I was at Staten Island for two weeks. I can remember standing below the Statue of Liberty looking up at it before we boarded the Queen Elizabeth. I was never scared about being in the war. I don't guess I ever really knew exactly why I was there. In the beginning when I was drafted, I thought they would put a gun in my hand and I'd start fighting right then. I had no clue or idea what it was all about. I remember trying to figure out how the Queen Elizabeth, with that much iron, and loaded with that many troops and that much equipment, could float on that water without sinking. I knew if I took an iron skillet and threw it out in the lake it would sink right then. And I haven't figured it out yet! I was thinking about how those six stories of metal could stay afloat when I walked up the gangplank to board the Queen Elizabeth. My quarters were down in the hull. They'd let us come up a few hours each day to the deck. I'd get off by myself and just stare out, still wondering about how that ship could stay on top of the water. I was plumb amazed. At this time, the Queen Elizabeth was the largest ship that floated. It took us six days to get from Staten Island to Glasgow, Scotland. We stayed at Glasgow until November 1943. Then we were moved to Southampton, England, where they lined us up on the beaches like seagulls, equipment and all, waiting on our orders.

Anybody could tell something was getting ready to happen if he just looked up at the sky. On June 4, 1944, there were so many airplanes and gliders overhead that they shut out the sun. It looked like a cloudy day. That went on for a couple of days, then the weather turned bad and very foggy. My outfit went to Normandy Beach in France on June 20, 1944, fourteen days after D-Day. We were on the beachhead for twenty-one days before our outfit could touch the ground. I was amazed to see so many apple trees in France. I was born and raised in the country and had never been anywhere before. There were apple trees lining both sides of the road as far as you could see.

I was under George S. Patton in the Third Army, in a combat engineer battalion attached to the Fifth Division. The military was not integrated then. The divisions were comprised of whites only. The coloreds were in companies or battalions attached to different divisions which were responsible for them. I was in three companies: the 438th Amphibian Duck, the 1354th Engineer Dump Truck, and the 1159th Combat Engineer. There were no coloreds qualified to take over a company of soldiers at that time. This didn't happen until after President Roosevelt when Harry S. Truman was elected President. There were a lot of white soldiers who had never seen a colored person until they got in the service. The colored soldiers had separate sleeping quarters from the whites, but when we came out to eat we all formed the mess line together.

When I was with the 1159th Combat Engineer Company, my duties were involved in the building of bridges. I rode in a patrol boat and put down the numbered sections which constructed the bridges. There were three boats on one side of the river, and three on the other side. We laid tracks across from one side to the other to make the bridge. There were two types of bridges.

One was the Bailey bridge made of fabricated steel lattices and wood; the other was a rubber pontoon bridge. This was how the tanks and trucks could get across the river.

I had three weapons. One was a fifty-seven machine gun 30-caliber, another was an M-1 rifle, and also a carbine rifle. Between building bridges, we saw some action. Whatever came along was what we had to do. We had to fight if it came to fighting. We had to defend ourselves. A lot of times, we would have to slip down undercover and start the bridges while the field artillery was firing over our heads. The longest Bailey bridge that was ever put across the Rhine River was put down by our company near Bonn, Germany.

After being out front for about ninety days, we'd get sent back to rest for a while. We'd get to change clothes and take a shower, maybe get our hair trimmed. One of the times when we went back, everybody was feeling good and celebrating. There was a boy from Oklahoma City named Willy B. Owens who got drunk. He said he could fly like one of the P-38 fighters. Nobody thought anything about what he was saying. They were just words. Somebody else said, "Oh, man, he can't fly." Another said, "Oh, yes he can. Jump!" And he did, right off the top of a two-story building. It didn't kill him right then. I don't know if it ever killed him. But he was hurt. They came and scooped him up and took him to the hospital, and there was never any more attention given to it than that. He wasn't crazy, just drunk. A lot of those guys after they got in there, and were in there for any length of time, got a little haggard, and just made up their minds that any way they could get out, they would.

I had some close calls. One time a grenade hit the back of a truck I was in and the truck exploded. A fragment hit and injured my elbow. It happened so fast, and I saw I was bleeding before I was aware of the injury. During the Battle of the Bulge, I was at Luxembourg when the Germans broke through. We had to back up the Fifth Division. We had to whitewash our trucks, tanks, guns, and bodies to camouflage them against the snow-covered ground. Everything that was moving had to be white. This was important if we needed to creep along in the snow at night to sabotage a bridge. It kept us from being seen. It was amazing to me that we would hear thunder, then it would cloud up and snow. Within twenty minutes the snow would be waist deep. It seemed the coldest place in the world.

There were mines everywhere. One could be inside a radish or a rutabaga, or even a dead bird along the side of the road. You had to constantly be on guard. And the guns were constantly firing... boom, boom, boom! That's what caused so many soldiers to get battle fatigue. You could be crawling along on your belly and see another soldier get blown up by a mine, and it would just run you nuts.

Each soldier got a ration of alcohol every month, one quart. Those who didn't drink it may have traded theirs for cigarettes. But I drank mine. Each soldier could also get a six-pack of beer in addition to the quart of whiskey. These alcohol rations would boost their morale up. They'd do just about anything to build their morale. That's what kept them going.

In April 1945, I left Europe from Le Havre, France. The plans were that I would be shipped to the South Pacific. We ran into a hurricane while we were on that small ship. Then was I scared! I got all the way through that other unafraid, and now I was really scared. I thought I was going to die, I was so seasick. But we made it back to Newport News, Virginia. Then I got to go home for a month. By the time I reported back to Fort Lewis, Washington, the war was over. It was September 1945 when I was discharged. The points system determined when I got out. There were two points for each year in, then three points for each battle star or anything outstanding, and about fifteen points just for being drafted into the service. It took me about two months to finally get out. I think it was fifty-two points.

After the war, the only thing I could look forward to was getting back to my family. I made it back home to Pickens, Arkansas, in January 1946, and that's where I've been ever since. My parents lived here. They came to Pickens in the late 1800s with their parents from Morehead Parish, Louisiana. I remember the day I got back home. My mother came running out crying and I told her we didn't need any of that now. I hadn't let her know I was coming. She said a spirit had told her I was coming. She had stopped what she was doing to walk to the back door and look out. That's when she saw me and ran out and grabbed me. She told me, "You know you can't slip up on me!" But, of course, that's just what I was trying to do. She said she had seen me in a dream the night before. She'd been looking for me all day. I didn't disappoint her. It's true: Nobody loves you like your mother. That's one thing I've taught my children, to respect their mother. They need to know the sacrifice a mother makes to bring them into this world.

I knew I wanted to come back home and farm on this plantation. I specialized in the motor patrol, keeping up the roads and cutting ditches. I ran the rows and leveled land. I operated and maintained the heavy equipment. Throughout the entire South, you won't find a better or finer plantation than the Pickens Farm. I've been here long enough to know.

One way the war affected my life was that it caused me to raise my kids better. Being in the war gave me greater respect for human beings and life itself. It was from having to see so many suffer and so many die. There was so much suffering in so many different ways. It made you want to find a good way for somebody else. I think about how much worse off I would have been if not for the war. I wouldn't have had any education, and probably wouldn't have had my jobs. And I might not have had my family, my twelve children. I don't want to brag too much on them, but they've all turned out intelligent with good enough sense. I always talked to my children. I looked them in the eyes and talked to them. They tell me I treated them like they were in the military. Maybe I learned that from the war! And three of my sons have chosen military careers.

I sat down and talked to my kids and told them the things I went through when I was young, like hand-picking and chopping cotton. You go out there and pick and chop cotton all day, from sunup to sundown. For seventy-five cents. I'm not talking about from eight o'clock in the morning until five o'clock in the afternoon. I'm talking about from daylight till dark. Seventy-five cents a day. First work I ever did in my life... here on this farm. I was nine years old. I worked Monday through Saturday. I didn't get the pay. My parents did. At the end of the week I might get thirty-five cents, and the rest would go for groceries or dry goods. After it got up to a dollar per day, then I got that money myself. I started getting paid a dollar per day when I was about fifteen years old, half grown. This was the way we worked during the harvest season, about two or three months each year usually during all of October and November.

There's one person in my life who has made a big difference to me and my family. Her name is Lois Brantley. She came to the Pickens Farm as a bookkeeper about two years after I got back from the war. Three years later, her father, Clarence Mahurin, became the Pickens Farm Manager. Miss Lois was always nice to us, just like a family person. She did us so many favors and helped us when we really needed it. She even did things for my dad. Anything about business my dad didn't understand, he went to Miss Lois.

Fred Henry Gordon, Sr.

Whatever she told you, it would be so. She voluntarily took our problems on her own. I could never thank her enough for everything. She was a woman no one could fool, really something else. One of my daughters is named for her. Miss Lois is someone we all look up to. And both Miss Lois and I are still right here on Pickens Farm. It's been more than fifty years.I wouldn't change anything at all about my life. But if I could change something about the world, it would be that people should try to be more understanding about each other. People ought to be willing to help one another and not make the other feel bad about it. Our faults should not disqualify us as human beings.

I never gave much thought about how I want to be remembered until I spent the last week in the hospital. And this is how I'd say it, "It ain't much, but I appreciate what I got." The night I came home from the hospital, my little five-year-old grandson sat next to me as I lay resting. He said, "Granddaddy, Granddaddy." And I told him to go on and let me rest. But he kept on trying to get my attention. He put his hand on top of my head, rubbing it, and saying, "Granddaddy, Granddaddy, you know what? I'm gonna be just like you." I just looked at him. I wondered what possessed him to come up with something like that. You just have to stop and listen to what the children are saying.

You've got to pay respect to education and patriotism. Education is what you've seen with your own eyes and experienced. No one can take that away from you. Each experience teaches you something new and different. Appreciate what you've got. Don't throw away or give away something that you've got. Take care of it. The war gave me both education and patriotism. I know what patriotism is and I know how to define it. It's what I have inside of me that makes me want to sit here and share my war stories with you. It's that something within your heart that made you come to listen.*

---

* author's footnote: Mr. Fred Henry Gordon died on February 1, 1999.

CHAPTER ELEVEN

ROY B. GREENLEE

DECEMBER 5, 1998

You know what I got for my first Christmas present overseas? A pair of Jap ears! But let me back up a little bit before I tell you about that...

I was in high school at Moore, Oklahoma, when I was drafted. I went to the draft board and told them I wanted to finish high school, which they allowed me to do. I had three months left before graduation. I wanted to be an aviator. I passed all the written examinations, but was refused because I was a little bit color blind. I wanted to be a pilot, but they said no, that I could be some other things. I decided if I couldn't be a pilot, then I'd join the army. Three of my buddies in high school got to be pilots, but not me. When I was barely nineteen years old, I left on a bus for Fort Sill, Oklahoma. I was there for about two weeks before they sent us by train to Camp Roberts, California. I was there for about nine months for basic training. I trained in communications and transportation automotive.

First, I went to Brisbane, Australia. I was in the replacements for the Forty-first Infantry Division. They had been fighting for about a year in New Guinea before I came in. We were the Sunset Division, MacArthur's Jungleers. I was in the Headquarters Company, First Battalion, 162nd Infantry. Our job was to keep communications between the higher echelon and the lower echelon. We went out on patrol with the line company to determine Japanese position. We strung low voltage wire between companies. The Japanese would jam our transmitters, so we had to go both ways. The Japanese would cut our wires, then wait on us to get there to fix them, and then shoot at us. The soldier in the rear who carried the receiver and transmitter on his back was always shot at by the Japanese. That soldier was protected very well. That soldier was me. I was the standout boy.

What beat the Japanese was our communications system. We had a lot better communications than they did. The Japanese had quality, but not quantity. Their receivers and transmitters were better than ours, but they didn't have enough of them. Our industry could provide fifty to every one of theirs.

The boys I was with were raised like me. They knew discipline and they were top quality people. One member of the signals crew operation named his first son after me, and I named mine after him. Both boys grew up to be ministers. Can you believe that?

Now, about that Christmas present... I met some real good Australian soldiers, and those Australians were fighters. They were like mountain men, just great fighters. They didn't like the Japanese at all. As long as I live, I will never forget that first Christmas present, courtesy of the Australians. It was a pair of Japanese ears! Sergeant Forbes was the one who actually wrapped them up in Christmas paper and gave them to me. Mostly, I think he just wanted to get my reaction. He really got me. It took a minute for me to figure out what they were, and I just about wanted to kill Forbes for it! You know what I mean. Everybody was getting Christmas presents coming in from home, when the sergeant gave me my present. That rascal! I'll never forget it.

In the jungles where I was, we had to wade in swamps and keep our guns way above the water level. It rained almost everyday. But it was one hundred-twenty degrees in the shade. High humidity. Insects. The biggest problems we had were disease and leaches. There were a lot of alligators, a lot of crocodiles. In Hollandia, New Guinea, we slipped off to go out and take a bath in the ocean. After about thirty minutes, we heard a scream from about a hundred yards out. One of the guys was under attack by a big crocodile. We couldn't do anything about it because we couldn't get there fast enough. He went under once, then twice. The third time we knew it would be over. So, one of the lieutenants picked up his rifle and killed the guy before he could go down the third time. It was a mercy killing. Not one of those guys ever went back in the water again. It was right before we went to Biak, and it's something I will never forget.

Bloody Biak was a battle that took about six weeks to secure the island. The units assembled to take Biak were called the Hurricane Task Force. The Japanese planned on using Biak to control the shipping and supply lanes from Australia north, out maybe five hundred miles back. The Japanese had two air fields there, and a third one in process of building. Early in the morning on my twenty-first birthday in 1944, it looked like the Fourth of July. The rockets, artillery, and airplanes all came in. Three battalions landed at one time. We thought we would take them easy, but we didn't.

This turned out to be the most expensive combat mission the Jungleers ever were to know- in length, strenuousness, and lives lost. Mokmer was the most important air drome, or air field, which needed to be taken first to conclude the New Guinea campaign. This was the assigned mission of the 162nd Infantry. When we landed on the beach, it took us about a day and a half to get a couple hundred yards into the area. It was intensely hot and humid. Troops were allowed only one canteen of water, which was most insufficient. They resorted to catching rain water in their ponchos. Lack of roads made getting supplies to them a problem.

Once we got in there, the 162nd Infantry met their first organized Jap resistance at a vertical coral and limestone cliff near Bosnek. General Douglas MacArthur ordered B-24s to fly over the high, narrow, and rocky ridges where the Japanese were hiding in caves, and for them to drop 155-gallon barrels of crude oil onto the cliffs. The oil went down in the crevices and to where the caves were, then our artillery shot in to set the oil afire. That was quite a sight! And all us guys were clapping and cheering because we'd fought those Japs left and right.

It was rough and it was bloody. The third day on Biak Island was the first time that the U.S. Army committed tanks over there- the first tank battle waged in the Pacific. I was within one hundred-fifty yards of that first tank battle. If I remember right, the Japanese had about fifty tanks and we had about eight. After it was over, seven Jap tanks lay completely destroyed on the beach and many others were severely damaged. Their tanks were no match for our Shermans. One hit from a Sherman, and they were gone. This was some of the hardest fighting our division did.

Colonel Archie Roosevelt was Theodore Roosevelt's oldest son. He was in the Third Battalion, same infantry. He took to me for some reason or other. He called me by my first name, never "Sergeant." My communications unit was attached to him and his unit all over the islands. His binoculars were superior to mine, and he let me use them to spot Japs. When I saw something, he called in the artillery for a couple of rounds, then that guy was gone. The Japanese would tie or hide themselves up in the coconut trees, and they were hard to see because they were camouflaged. They might kill twenty troops before we got them. And they didn't care if they died themselves. That's just the way they fought. Once we were walking in a broom corn field, and the guy walking in front of me was shot right through the head by one of those Jap snipers. He was right in front of me!

When we got out of Biak, we went to Leyte for about two weeks and mopped up, then to Luzon for about ten days. By March, we were in Zamboanga City on Mindanao in the southern Philippines. We fought there for almost four months before we were able to bivouac. We had to defeat the enemy before we could have a resting period. Then we resumed training for almost three months for the landing on the mainland of Japan.

We weren't allowed to eat any food except military meals. When we were bivouaced, we ate two meals a day. But we ate hardtack and hoped for C-rations when we were fighting. I lived on one of those hardtack boxes of K-rations many times. You could eat one of those "candy bars" and drink some canteen water, and that would buy you a day. It was full of energy, and tasted good, too. The C-rations were really great. Oh, man, canned beef and canned vegetables! We thought we were in hog heaven. We robbed what the Japs had in their supplies, but it was mostly rice. In my tent, I kept three or four stalks of bananas at various stages of ripeness. Since I didn't smoke, I traded my cigarettes to get those bananas. I got to where I didn't like to go to the mess hall because I didn't like that food. So, I ate a lot of bananas and other fresh fruits.

In Zamboanga City, we had a dance one night. I played the Dobro, a little steel lap guitar, and several of my company came. That's where we first saw people eating unhatched eggs. These were eggs that had little chickens in them, and they would crack them open and eat it raw. Now, I could not do that. It was a delicacy to those people. Man, they went wild over those things! I saw a lot of things like that over there, but it was just a different kind of culture.

Some of the American soldiers would go out looking for war souvenirs. One popular item was Japanese teeth. If they'd been caught at it, they would have been court-martialed, but the commanders couldn't keep up with all the details of what was going on. When the Japanese realized what the

Americans were doing, they began booby-trapping their dead bodies with mines. It caused some American soldiers to be blown up. It's absolutely true. The Japs booby-trapped all kinds of things. You had to watch out for everything. I wouldn't touch anything for fear of being blown up. Nothing was worth taking that chance.

I was in many banzai attacks. The banzai soldier was ready and willing to die for the Emperor, and he wasn't trained to think for himself. We were vulnerable in our position because we didn't have front line fighting. We could be approached and attacked from many sides because everything was circular perimeters. The Japanese company commander got his soldiers drunk on saki, then sent them to our camp on a suicide murder mission. They broke through our outposts between two and three o'clock in the morning, usually when it was raining so we couldn't hear them coming. I kept about thirty Australian grenades with me in the foxhole. I thought those were superior grenades to ours because they broke up into more pieces than the American grenades. I threw those things many a time at night when I heard the banzais coming. If we heard someone sneaking around outside the foxhole, we knew it was them because the rule among ourselves was to never get out of the foxhole at night. When I got up the next morning, I'd see as many as ten young dead Japanese soldiers lying right in front of my foxhole.

The first thing to do when we knew we were staying some place overnight, was to dig a foxhole. The terrain might be sandy or rocky. Sometimes we were lucky to get down twelve inches. In that case, we had to build up a bank around it. It was the only protection we had. In my foxhole at night, I had to have a flashlight so I could see the keys to send out communications in Morse code. We had four-letter codes which changed everyday. The lieutenant would tell us verbally about the code changes. That was part of our communication system that beat the Japanese. We could decipher their messages, but they couldn't ours. We outsmarted them.

After the atomic bombs were dropped on Hiroshima and Nagasaki, Japan surrendered. I stayed on after that for communications. We went all over the island and saw defensive implacements with big rifle guns, bigger than we had on our battleships. They were on tracks. The Japs were ready for us. There would have been a lot of our troops killed if we had not dropped those atomic bombs. I went to see Hiroshima about six weeks after the bomb was dropped. Three-quarters of a mile all around from where that bomb was dropped, there was nothing left. The steel structures were melted just like a huge welding torch had been put to them. They were completely burned down. As we went further out, the damage became less and less. I had a chance to go to Nagasaki, but I had seen all I wanted to see in Hiroshima.

At the end of the war, I couldn't go home right away because I didn't have enough points. I had the chance to go to Australia for nine months of lieutenant officer's training which would have lead to missile development, but I declined because I wanted to go back home and attend college. I had my mind made up that I wanted to get my degree. While in the war, I took math correspondence courses sent to me by the University of Oklahoma. I carried those text books around with me everywhere I went. I mailed in the answers, then waited for them to send me the next course. I completed the courses when I didn't have anything else to do. I kept up with the business of the war first, but that study project sometimes helped me keep my sanity. I told them I loved my country, but I wanted out of this war and to get back home and go to college. I've often wondered if I would have been better off to go to Australia and get that training, but I didn't do it. I eventually got my degree in civil engineering from the University of Oklahoma.

* * *

My dad fought in World War I, and he told me what the Germans in the military did in the countries they occupied, like killing people for no reason. Dad taught me what a great country we have as far as liberty is concerned. Each one of us in this country has more liberty than any other country in the world. I've always loved my country. I studied history in high school, and often history brings these things out. In high school, I was president of my class for three years, and I played football. These were opportunities I was appreciative of. When I got into the service, I had a new world to live in, but everything pointed to the right or the wrong. I wanted to fight the Japanese to keep them from coming over here to our country, and I was determined that they would never take me alive. After seeing some of the world, like Japan and Australia, I knew they didn't have it like our country. They didn't have the privacy we do, and they had laws I didn't like. In the Philippines, they hardly had communication among themselves, and they had poor schooling. Stop and think about the industry in our country. We have been able to use our natural resources and pass them along to the consumer. Our technology has always been better than other countries, and it continues to be. All these factors add up to why I love my country. It isn't perfect, but I still love it. I think it's the best country in the world.

Everything goes back to the family home. In the early 1930s, my father worked in the oil fields around Seminole, Oklahoma. When he got his check, he would give half that money to my mother for the survival of our family, which included seven children. The other half he used to buy groceries for families he knew who were starving and really needed food. I saw what he did, and it weighed on me. I took that philosophy from my dad and went through life with it.

Children today lack the type of discipline like I had growing up. Both their parents are off working, and the children have to stay home by themselves. And that's when I got in trouble as a child, when my parents weren't around. As children grow up, there is a lot they don't know about life. They need their parents to be there to teach them those things. The parents need to be there to help the children make up their minds about things, not just go out on their own. Children need the voice of reason.

Dad was a professional boxer as a young man. When I was a boy, I went to school with many Seminole Indian boys who whipped up on me all the time. Dad said he was going to put a stop to that, and he bought me a pair of boxing gloves. He spent the summer teaching me how to box. I got to where I could handle those bullies pretty well. I didn't have any more trouble. They didn't bother me anymore. See, Dad knew what to do for me to help me out. That's what makes a good family.

Some of my heroes were Joe DiMaggio, Gene Autry, and Roy Rogers. And Bud Wilkinson, the University of Oklahoma football coach, was a great man to me. When I look back on the military, there were two generals I thought were tops: Douglas MacArthur, who saved the lives of so many men by the way he handled things in the Pacific, and Rommel of Germany, who was a strategist and didn't just take his troops out to be killed. I have read the histories of these two men, and I idolize them.

There's one thing I might have changed about my life if I could. Instead of being so involved in the technicalities of my field, I might have been in the management end of it. Then I would have delegated more of the activities so that I could have done other things, like go fishing more!

Roy B. Greenlee

I've been fortunate to have all the money I need; I'm not a greedy person. I have a sweet wife, good kids, a pretty nice home, a fine bass boat, and a good truck. It's not that I've been smart, just lucky. I would like to be remembered as a man who enjoys doing things that help others get along, expecting nothing in return. I've got everything I need, so why not give something back? God gave us a brain to use and He expects us to use it to make these kinds of decisions about how we live our lives. I've just always tried to live my life doing unto others as I would have them do unto me. If you do that, at least you'll almost always come out even.

CHAPTER TWELVE

W. BRYAN HALEY

JULY 30, 1998

I was at my fiancée's home in McGehee, Arkansas, when I heard about Pearl Harbor, on December 7, 1941. We heard it on the radio. We'd been hearing about the Japanese and Americans squabbling back and forth, but everybody thought it would be settled. We didn't think the Japanese would do anything, besides we knew we could whip the Japanese in a couple of hours at the most. But everybody got fooled.

I didn't have any feelings about the war one way or another. Nobody knew anything about a war. I didn't know if I would ever get to a war or not. In April 1942, it hadn't gotten to that stage. In the 1930s and 1940s, nobody knew what a war was, or what it took to fight a war, or how many people would be killed.

Before we left on the invasion, I was at a big speech given by General Patton in Wolverton, England. I couldn't tell you what he said, except that every other word was a curse word. He was all dressed up. We were in his division at that time, the Third Army. That's the only time I ever saw him. Then I was transferred to the First Army and we went to Cardiff, Wales. From there, we went to Normandy, France.

I was twenty-nine years old when I landed at Utah Beach on June 8, 1944. I was part of the Fourth Division with the Ninetieth Battalion. We went in behind the Eighty-second Airborne to relieve them. When I got there, shelling was still going on. Machine guns were firing on the beach.

The USS Arkansas and USS Texas battleships were to our right firing into the land.

Where we went through, on both sides of the road there were fields full of poles placed there by the Germans. When the P-47s had brought in our gliders and cut them loose, the poles caught their wings and caused them to wreck. There were dead men lying all around where they'd hit. One of the first ones I saw, everybody in the glider had been killed. Some of them were lying on the outside, and the rest were inside. Another I saw was partially burned. There were a bunch of those things. As we went on through, we saw the dead men of the Eighty-second Airborne being laid side by side in rows. A big truck would come along and pick them up. There was truckload after truckload. I had seen some casualties on the beach, but nothing like this. We went on past Saint Mere-Eglise. We saw more of the dead paratroopers from the Eighty-second Airborne. They were scattered everywhere. They lost a lot of their men. I thought that wouldn't happen to me. I thought things would be different for me. Even though it happened to another person, it wouldn't happen to me. A lot of people back at that time wondered what we were doing over there. Nobody really knew. Nobody knew what was going on in Germany. We never saw a concentration camp. We were so busy trying to stay alive, we didn't have a lot of time to think about why we were there.

We started fighting in the late afternoon of June 10. But we didn't really get into it until the morning of June 11. On that day, we lost ninety-nine men from our company. Some were killed, some wounded, some captured. We'd had about one hundred-eighty men to start with, so that meant we'd lost half our company on the first day. Replacements started coming in pretty quick.

The Germans were professional fighters. They'd been fighting for years and knew all about it. The Germans had been in France for a long time. They knew the country and had their guns set up in certain positions. It limited our progress. There were just certain ways we could go. The fields were covered with hedgerows and the only way to get through was to blow a hole in it, or run a tank through it. The hedgerows were tall and thick. The Germans expected us to try to use the roads, and had their guns set up for it. They had the high ground. They could watch everything we did. It seemed like the Germans knew all the answers, and we didn't even know the questions.

* * *

I got hit December 10, 1944. I was across the Saar River, just into Germany, and it was snowing. It was a mortar shell or artillery shell that hit me. I never heard it. When I came to, I was lying on the ground. There were other men around me. One man right next to me was killed instantly. I broke both legs in multiple places, my arm and wrist, and my hip. Medics were sent in. Some German prisoners carried me down to a little building. Then I was taken down to the river, and they put some stretchers across a boat and carried me across that way. Then I was put on a Jeep and taken to a hospital. I don't remember if I was in pain. They gave me morphine. Maybe I was in shock. The weather was pretty cold. One man being wounded didn't mean anything.

The hospital I was taken to was in Thionville, France, south of Luxembourg. They patched me up and took me to an airfield to fly me back to the United States or England. I was there for two days, then all the airplanes were grounded due to bad weather. So I was put on a train, an old freight car with decks made to put people on. I was taken to Paris where we were fed and bathed, and stayed a couple of days. From there we went to Cherbourg, France, and then on a boat to Southampton, England.

I got to the hospital in England on Christmas Eve day. That's when we heard all about the Battle of the Bulge. I was there until March 20, when I was taken to Charleston, South Carolina, and then New Orleans, Louisiana. Finally, I was in San Antonio, Texas, where I stayed until the next March 1945. I was in all these different hospitals for about sixteen months. The first time I got out of bed was in July 1945. When I tried to stand up, I couldn't. It was a shock. But, being young, I was able to recover. I got a furlough in August.

Since I was in the war, I've had four operations on one of my legs, and six additional operations. I've had a total of eleven operations including the one they did on me in the war.

After forty-some-odd years, it all just kind of slips away a little bit at a time. Every now and then I'll think about something I haven't thought about in forty years. Then I forget again. But I never really forget, having gone through it. What I've run into is that many men who came back try to remember the humorous things that happened. I, too, can remember some things I thought were humorous, even though it was in the middle of a war. I can remember those times easier than I can remember some other things. One time we took a town after the breakthrough at St-Lo. There were tanks mixed in with our trucks as we were going down the road, and there were Jeeps and other vehicles with machine guns on them. We were spearheading the drive. When we ran into anything coming down the road, we'd all get off the road and start fighting. We went through the town. It was deserted and there was no one to give us any problems. Then we ran into some Germans who were drunk on cognac. It was getting late. The Germans were still drinking and having a big time. They didn't concern us too much. We decided to spend the night. At daybreak, we got word that some Germans had moved back into the town we'd passed through the day before. The next troop of Americans who came through were attacked and about to lose. They called for us to come back and help them. When we jumped on our vehicles and started going back toward the town, the drunken Germans thought we were running from them, and began chasing after us. Their cannons and all their equipment were horsedrawn. Of course, they couldn't keep up. When we got to the town, another outfit had come and helped out, so we weren't needed. We turned around to go back the other way, and ran into those drunken Germans. We blew them off the road with our tanks before they had time to think about it.

Another time, a German tank came down the road just as it was getting dark. Some of our tanks were there. The German tank parked right in the middle of our tanks without even knowing it. He didn't find out until the next morning when he woke up. He was in shock because he'd thought those were all German tanks.

There was an old boy from Iowa. He was about forty years old and could have gotten out of going to the war, but he didn't want to. When we first got to France, around June 11, it was just getting dark. He came up to me and asked, "Who's on our left?" I said the Germans. He said, "Who's on our right?" I said the Germans. He said, "Who's on the front?" I said the Germans. He said, "Well, where the hell's everybody we're supposed to have?" I said there was nobody there but us. All he could do was walk away.

There was a German airplane that came over us right off the beach when we were first there. He'd come over at night, and every now and then he'd drop a few bombs. Then he'd fly back. We called him "Bed-check Charley" because he always flew over us when it was time to go to sleep. We'd have to run for cover every time. We didn't want to stir up anything at night if we could keep from it, so we didn't take any action against him.

We were so tired at night. We slept in the same heavy clothes we'd worn all day. There were usually two men to a foxhole. One would sleep three hours, then the other would sleep three hours.

One time they pulled us off the front. Where we went it was a hard surface. I told the men to "dig in." They all grumbled about it because the ground was so hard. Right away, some shells hit in a field next to us. It wasn't two minutes before they all had their foxholes dug. That'll sure make you dig a hole!

A few times, the kitchen unit came up behind us and served us a hot meal, but that wasn't very often. We usually carried rations on us. Sometimes we had to stock up for two days or so. But when we had to run through a field and then land on our stomachs, those cans would be thrown this way and that way. Nobody wanted to land on a can and break a rib when he hit the ground.

There were always plenty of cigarettes. Everybody smoked them because they were there and they were free. They would have huge piles of them by the cartons. Every ration we'd open up would have cigarettes in it. Every time we stopped, we'd all light up a cigarette. Back home at that time, a package of cigarettes cost twenty cents. One time I ran into some Frenchmen who offered me twenty dollars for a carton of cigarettes. Our cigarettes were so much better than theirs. Theirs were like smoking corn shucks. I didn't sell them, though, mainly just because I didn't want them to have any.

When we went in, each soldier was given currency called invasion money. It was printed up by the government and it was French money. They didn't want us to go into the country and just take things. They wanted us to be able to pay for what we needed. I never spent mine. I gave it away after I got back home.

* * *

The war changed the course of my life in some ways. It was bound to. It changed everybody's way of thinking. Everything was so different after that. From the time the war started, up until now, things have been affected by the war. The war made for more changes than would have happened otherwise. It changed our way of living as far as income. Back then, twenty dollars a week was considered a living. You could take three dollars and fill up a grocery cart. A work week was generally six days a week, from seven o'clock in the morning until six o'clock in the afternoon. That made for about ten cents an hour. The war changed our economy and more. Automobiles changed completely; homes changed completely; the way you dressed, the way you ate, everything- it all changed. It changed everything in the world, and for the better. We wouldn't have had televisions or air conditioners otherwise. The war elevated us from that low level of earning power. It made dreams possible.

Being in the war made me realize that I could do more than I had been doing before the war. I came back and went to business school and got into accounting. I established my own business. If it hadn't been for the war, I would have never done that. Before the war, when I was in high school, we didn't have the opportunity to learn typing or bookkeeping. About the only choice was to go get a job in a store, or do farming. And farming at that time was really hard work. I'd hardly left my hometown before the war. When I got in the army, I began traveling all over. That changed my perspective. Before the war, not many students got to go to college after high school because the money wasn't available. When the war was over, the colleges were full of G.I.s with the government paying their way.

We never thought much about patriotism in the late 1930s. Most of the boys joined the army or the navy because they wanted a job to get some money, not because they were patriotic. We didn't think there was anything going on to be patriotic about. Some boys who hadn't wanted to join the service changed their minds when they knew there was fighting going on. Then they wanted to go because they had the urge to find out what it was all about. You have to develop a sense of patriotism. It's a feeling for your country because it's the best there is. You wouldn't trade it for anything in the world. Even though there are things that seem wrong, it doesn't mean you'd want to make a big change.

At certain times and certain stages in my life, I've had various heroes. When I was a kid, Babe Ruth and Lou Gehrig were my heroes. I always thought of General Robert E. Lee as a hero. These were people I admired. Having a hero, or someone to look up to, can keep someone from getting into trouble. It keeps a mind off the wrong things.

I'm glad I wasn't born when things are like they are now. It's tough on a kid these days, especially in cities. They have to face whether or not to join a gang, and either way it's tough on them. There wasn't any such thing as a gang when I was a kid. If there was, it didn't amount to anything. We may

W. Bryan Haley

have had a group of three or four boys who might fight among themselves, but that was it.

Used to, when I was growing up, our whole family sat down at one time together and ate our meals. Everybody would be discussing everything. We had a lot of time to spend together. It brought a closeness to our family. Back in those days, we didn't have a car to be running around in. There wasn't any place to go. We might walk downtown for a few minutes and then come back home. Now, the way the kids run around, it seems they might not see their folks for a day or two. And they're missing out on something. Home is where you get your values. Some kids get started off on the wrong foot, and pick up a bad friend here and there, and they just never can get straightened out after that.

I hope when people remember me, they'll think, "He was a good old boy." I don't know if I have done anything in particular to be remembered for. That kind of thing doesn't happen to most people. Most people just live an ordinary, normal life. You don't have to do or accomplish some big something to be a success. If you have a happy family, and if you help somebody when you can, that helps you to be a success.[*]

[*] author's footnote: Mr. W. Bryan Haley died on February 3, 1999.

CHAPTER THIRTEEN

WILLIAM PLEASANT HOLLAND

NOVEMBER 18, 1998

I didn't volunteer. They drafted me. That was in 1942, and I got out in 1947. I was in the Third Army, the Eighty-fourth Division of the Infantry, the Rail-Splitters.

We went to France after D-Day. When we landed over there, it was ice-cold, and we had to wade in waist-deep water getting off the ship. We thought the Germans would be there, but they weren't. They had already moved out. We were on trucks at first, then when we got to the front line we had to walk. Some soldiers' feet became frozen so hard, they had to have them amputated. It didn't happen to me, maybe because I was walking all the time. You had to keep moving. I didn't sleep much during that time. Sometimes I might get to take a little nap in the foxhole, but they pretty much kept us awake. When we were in basic training, it took a half day to dig a foxhole, but when we got in the war, it only took a few minutes. When all those bullets and bombs are coming in on you, it doesn't take you long to get your head down in the dirt. I had worked on a farm all of my life, and I was good and stout. If I hadn't been, I couldn't have taken being in the war.

We kept going with K-rations. It was just a block of something to eat. I don't know what was in it, but it would sure keep you going. Sometimes we went a couple of days without water. Sometimes we went without K-rations, too. The supply unit couldn't always keep up. That old boy who drove the K-rations truck was scared having to drive through bullets. He was from

Alabama and he told us those bullets were saying that he was never going back to Alabama. In a way, he was in worse danger than any of us. At least we could get down flat. He was a good target up high in that truck.

After we got into Germany, the Germans got so hot after us that we had to withdraw and go back. We swam across a river as we moved forward, then had to turn around and swim right back across it with the Germans after us.

Our lieutenants really ate us up during basic training and up until the time we got into action, but when those bullets started flying, they puppied down. Some of them stood up to it, like the head of my company, Lieutenant, later Captain, George Geisel. He wouldn't tell you to do anything he wouldn't do himself. Then there was Sergeant Searcy. He was a tough old guy who had been in the army fifteen years. When the war started, he thought he knew it all. And he was probably right. If we did anything wrong, he really cussed us out. One time Sergeant Searcy came into the camp when they had just started building it. It was Saturday evening and we were all sitting in a room. He asked for volunteer truck drivers. Most of them went because they wouldn't mind driving a truck. Three or four of us stayed in the barracks. Sergeant Searcy came to me and asked why I didn't volunteer. I told him I didn't even volunteer for the army, and I wasn't volunteering for anything else. The ones who had volunteered as truck drivers ended up hauling gravel in wheel barrows in order to build a sidewalk, so I was happy about my decision.

While we were in Belgium, I remember seeing General Patton with his pearl-handled pistols. He eventually took over our outfit. He was up at the front line with us much of the time. He was a brave old fellow.

Our company had a bad job there for a week or two. We were the clean-up guys behind the lines. We had to clean up everything as we went. This meant gathering up stray German soldiers who were left behind. We weren't looking for wounded or dead Germans. We were searching for live ones. One night we came upon a house. We could hear Germans down in the basement and we had to go down there and get them. But they gave up right quick not knowing how much we had outside, which was only seven or eight men. They didn't want to fight any more than we did. The ones we found were taken back and put in prison. At least most made it to the prison. Sometimes the Germans would be killed before they made it to the prison.

One night I was out on guard and some Germans came by. They were pretty close. I hollered for them to halt, and they ran. Since they ran, I fired at them. We were not allowed to fire if they didn't run. I don't know if I killed any of them or not.

Another time we captured some Germans and it began to rain. We took shelter in a building, but the Germans were made to stay out in the rain as we kept watch on them. Still another time, we were in an old house, and we could hear a German hollering from another house. He was hollering like that because he was wounded. So, we went there and got him and put him out in the rain. We took turns guarding him through the night.

One time we were out on patrol behind the German lines. We had drunk a lot of whiskey before we left. As we walked through the woods, the Germans opened up fire on us. One of the men in our group was a big Indian fellow. He was from Oklahoma and we called him "Chief." When we got fired at, we took off running back to the line, all except the big Indian. He didn't show up for another thirty minutes. He told us he had picked up the body of a dead German and put it over him until they stopped firing. It was no trouble to find a dead German lying around.

I remember there was a woman sniper, a German soldier, up in a two-story house out on a porch, and she hit two or three of our guys. One of our boys had a bazooka and he shot her with it. Another dead German.

If a buddy got wounded, we were not allowed to stop and help him. We just had to leave him hollering. We hated to do it, but we had to. More of us would have gotten killed if we'd stopped to help. The medics were supposed to come along and do that. There were also people who came along behind us and picked up the dead bodies. As the replacement troops came in, I learned not to get acquainted with them. Soon, most of them would be killed or wounded. Then the next group of men would arrive. Not many of my original outfit got back from the war.

I got hit just before we made it to the Rhine River. It was just before Thanksgiving, and I was in the foxhole, probably as good a one as we ever had, and they threw an 88 in on me. I still have scars on my hands and knees and the back of my head where the steel went through my helmet. I had shrapnel under my kneecap for almost two weeks after that. I was hurt real bad, and it killed the guy, Goins, who was in there with me. It happened at three o'clock in the morning. They got me out of there and took me into an old house. At daylight they put me on a Jeep, and the bombing started again.

So, I got out of the Jeep and crawled under it. The company commander came out and told the Jeep driver to get me back on that Jeep and get the hell out of there.

Back in England at the hospital, when they operated on me, they didn't deaden my knee. A big female nurse sat on me, and that old doctor cut the shrapnel out. He didn't even give me a shot, no anesthesia. They would have sent me back into action after I got better, but that old doctor wouldn't let me even walk. He kept me in a wheelchair.

* * *

When I knew I was going into the war, I wasn't worried. I was kind of glad when we went. When we weren't in a battle, it was better to be over in Europe than home in the United States. When we had time off, it was really time off. Back home on the farm we never got a rest like that.

I had to go there and defend my country to keep those Germans from coming over here. I couldn't have gotten out of going to the war, so I may as well have liked going, but I was afraid all the time I was over there. Some of the soldiers would tell you they weren't scared, but they'd be telling you a story. The ones who got too scared probably got themselves killed that way. I guess I was less scared than some. I was always praying for my life.

One thing I never understood about that war is that the fighting would stop in order to let both sides collect their dead, then they'd start fighting again. It didn't make sense to me. It looks like if you could stop it like that, then you could stop it for good.

I thought we did a good job in the war. But the bad thing about war is how it makes you care less for yourself and others. I was just proud to get back alive. When we went overseas they told us they were giving us a one-way ticket. That didn't give us much hope. I thought for sure it was the end of everything when I jumped off in that waist-deep freezing water off the coast of France. That turned out not to be so bad at all compared to what it was on the front line.

When I got back from the war, I had trouble sleeping. It lasted a good while. It took a year or two to wear off. My wife said I called out during my sleep, "Look out! Here it comes! Get out of the way!" I guess I was dreaming.

William Pleasant Holland

I feel like all of us who came back from that war were heroes. But the biggest hero to me was our Captain Geisel. I learned an important lesson from him which I've tried to apply in my life, and that's to never ask anyone else to do something I wouldn't do myself.

I think I've been a pretty good guy and I hope that's the way people will remember me. The bravest thing I ever did in my life was go fight that war. I'd like to be remembered as a man who helped save our country, and one who would do anything to help an old soldier.

CHAPTER FOURTEEN

ROBERT ORBACH

OCTOBER 6, 1998

I was born and raised in Oklahoma City. I attended the University of Oklahoma and was in advanced ROTC. I graduated in the Class of 1942. Unfortunately, I did not get my commission in the field artillery from the University of Oklahoma because for some odd reason I had not had summer camp which was part of the training in order to get a commission. There were about sixty of us throughout the United States in similar circumstances who had not had summer camp. We found ourselves at Fort Sill, and the army didn't know what to do with us. We were civilians who had not been enlisted in the army. For about a week they had us doing all sorts of details that had nothing to do with the army, in our civilian clothes, the very clothes we had worn to come down there. After a week, we were pretty filthy as you might imagine. They decided they'd put us in Officer Candidate School. In those days, Officer Candidate School was comprised of regular army sergeants, master sergeants, whatever. Some were men returned from their campaign in North Africa, all were people who had been in the army for many years. They took one look at sixty college boys, all twenty-one years old with no experience whatsoever, who knew nothing about the army, about marching, about drill, about anything, and here we were thrown in with them in the Twentieth Class of Officer Candidate School. I've always said we grew up in a hurry. We had not only to absorb everything we didn't know, but we had to conduct ourselves along a tight line rope, not acting too smart due to our college background, but not acting too dumb either. We had to really carry it off. Well, not all of us made it. Fortunately, I was one of the few who did survive that, and did get my commission as a second lieutenant in the field artillery.

My first duty assignment after being commissioned a second lieutenant was with the First Cavalry Division at Fort Bliss, Texas. That sort of sounded like fun, and it was - until I got there and found out that the First Cavalry was still horse cavalry. It was the only horse cavalry division left in the United States Army. It was a regular army division. The mission that the First Cavalry thought they would have, no matter how long the war would last, was to guard the Mexican border which they could do best with horses. Every week we would go out into the desert around Fort Bliss and train with those horses for three days, then we would come in and spend two days cleaning up the harnesses, cleaning up the horses, and acting like there was no war at all. This, or course, made no sense whatsoever.

One very dismal day, in came hundreds of immense trucks. Before the day was over, there was not a horse left on the post. All these horses had been hauled away. And the army, in its infinite wisdom, had turned the First Cavalry Division into an armored unit. Most of the enlisted men who were in that division didn't even know how to drive an automobile. They did not know anything about anything mechanized. They were all regular army personnel. The enlisted men who were horseshoers were turned into motor sergeants when they couldn't even drive a car. It was the biggest mess you ever did see. Obviously, I lived through that, and very shortly was assigned to a field artillery unit that was not part of the First Cavalry, and thus began my military career.

We trained at the usual long and varied number of military posts in the United States. It seemed like every few months we were moved to somewhere else. But we trained, and we trained hard. We trained in Tennessee Maneuvers two times, back to back. If the war had been as bad as Tennessee Maneuvers, we never would have won it. Tennessee Maneuvers made you grow up in a hurry, and grow up hard. It was cold, and there was no getting out of the rain or the snow. And there was the aggravation. It was intense, intense, intense. We became a very, very tough bunch of people. It was difficult. We didn't know it but we were destined to be part of General Patton's Third Army in the European Theater.

We went to England right after the Normandy Invasion, June 1944. Then we went to Wales. We received all our equipment and began training again. We were being held back, waiting until enough forces accumulated to start the Third Army on its way, and waiting for the breakthrough out of Normandy. The breakthrough occurred early in August 1944. As soon as it looked like this was to be accomplished, we were on ships crossing the English Channel. We landed at Omaha Beach, unloaded, and we were in combat within twenty-four hours, taking casualties. We became the support field artillery headquarters group of the Fourth Armored Division which was the spearhead of General Patton's Third Army. We fought with the Fourth Armored Division and the Third Army from Normandy to Czechoslovakia. We were never out of combat a single day. We relieved Bastogne, and were part of the fun and frolic of the dash across France. We were on the east side of Paris when Paris fell. We were supposed to take Paris, but at the last minute they decided to let Generals DeGaulle and LeClerc of the French retake Paris. Our mission was to shoot up the Germans who were fleeing Paris. Our artillery was deadly and we inflicted immense casualties on the Germans as they were running out of Paris.

From there we continued the fight across France until such time as we ran out of gas and ammunition. There was an immense disagreement between General Eisenhower and General Patton about the call for supplies, men, and materiel on the part of General Montgomery who wanted the honor of winning the war. Obviously, General Patton wanted the honor for himself. So, we were caught like sitting ducks with no ammunition, no gasoline, and no way of moving while all this argument took place. At this point, the Germans finally caught onto the fact that there was something wrong because we had simply stopped. The Germans counter-attacked. Our most serious engagement was at a little village near Nancy, France. We were counter-attacked by three Panzer divisions. We took immense casualties.

One of my soldiers was Corporal Knopf who had come into our field artillery group as a replacement directly from Ohio State University where he had completed his sophomore year. He was the battery clerk. I kept in touch with Corporal Knopf sporadically over the years after the war. He wrote to me early this past summer to share with me a letter he'd written to Senator John Glenn of Ohio.

The letter told the senator that I, Lieutenant Robert Orbach, had suffered a grave oversight during the war. On September 24, 1944, during the Battle of France, Colonel Richard Guthrie and I had directed the artillery fire from the same foxhole against a Panzer division and had inflicted tremendous casualties upon them. Hundreds of American lives were saved. I had maintained communications from that same foxhole we shared.

Colonel Guthrie was awarded the Silver Star for his heroic act, but I was overlooked and had not been awarded anything. The colonel and I were the only survivors out of this particular engagement. Now Professor Knopf thought something should be done about it. I received a letter from the War Department stating that they would make a decision between the next eighteen to twenty-four months. It would be an honor to receive such an award, but I feel equally honored that an enlisted man thought that much of me, his officer, to raise this issue after fifty-four years.

We relieved the last village to fall in the European Theater in World War II, Strakonice, Czechoslovakia, south of Prague. The Czechs were being massacred in Prague by the Germans during the last days of the war. Here we were, less than an hour away, with enough ammunition and supplies, to be there within an hour or two to stop this massacre. What we did not know, and what the Czechs did not know, was that at the conference in Yalta in February, 1945, it had been agreed that the Americans would stop and let the Russians take Prague and Czechoslovakia. This was a heart-rending thing because we were in contact with the Czechs by radio, and could hear, "Come, come, come...." and that they were being killed without mercy. Here we sat just an hour away and could have stopped it.

As we came into Strakonice, a very old man, climbed up on my vehicle. He presented me with a plaque that he had made during the German occupation. He'd written on the back of it in Czech, "In commemoration of the liberation of Strakonice on the 6th of May, 1945 by the American troops." Of course, the war wasn't over until the 8th of May, but we had sat there for two days waiting for the war to be over. The Czech population treated us like absolute royalty. They brought us food and surrounded our command post with Czech old men and boys with their swords, butcher knives, and guns which they'd saved away from the Germans. They were there to guard us. No longer did we have to post guards because we had a man every six feet, twenty-four hours a day. The Germans were coming in by the thousands. One vehicle would be pulling two or three. Some would be walking. These were the Germans fleeing the Russians.

* * *

Not many German airplanes were shot down by an armored division. They were usually pretty hard to hit with fifty-caliber machine guns. And there wasn't much left of the Luftwaffe anyway when we broke out of Normandy in 1944. But the steady gunners of the Fourth Armored Division managed to bag a big one very early one morning. It turned out to be one hell of a problem. As was custom, the tanks and artillery would form a giant circle at night which would uncoil in the morning when we went back on the attack. This was a pretty sound defensive measure except it made us very vulnerable to an air assault. That's why all hell broke loose when a large, and unmistakably German plane flew right over the bivouac at dawn. There was a roar as hundreds of antiaircraft machine guns fired tracers at this big bird as it lumbered across our area at about one thousand feet altitude. How most of them missed was remarkable. The plane, which was a Fokker transport, about the size of an old Ford Tri-motor, a very small transport plane, came gliding down with only a few holes in the wing. It was loaded with German nurses who were being evacuated from Brittany and not a one of them was hurt, but they were plenty scared. This was the first time we'd captured any nurses. And though we were capturing a lot of soldiers everyday, no one knew quite what to do with this plane load of frauleins. Intelligence contacted Third Army headquarters about the problem. We were advised to put them in a truck and haul them with us until there was an open evacuation route to take them to the rear. And that's just what we did. I'll bet those babes never forgot their tour through France with the Fourth Armored Division which was on the attack.

* * *

During the Battle of the Bulge, our artillery people were able to get out of the snow by staying in houses because we weren't moving all the time. The infantry took the brunt of sleeping in the snow and freezing. I found a place in a cellar in a home in a little town in Luxembourg. I bedded down on a pile of sugar beets which they used to feed the cattle. The woman of the house was there and it was almost Christmas. She decided she would make a Christmas cake for the soldiers staying in her house who were defending her country. She began to make it when suddenly we got a fire mission. We had a battalion of field artillery right across the street from her house. They all started shooting at the same time. You can imagine what happened to her cake. It was in the oven of a wood-fired stove, and it went flat as a pancake. The lady cried her eyes out. But we had a hell of a time. She had a lot of wine stashed and that helped.

* * *

By the time the Germans broke through for the Battle of the Bulge, I was a first lieutenant and a fairly important cog in the machine. The colonel called me in one morning and said to get ready to go on reconnaissance. I knew we weren't going on reconnaissance because we were in a position that was very, very close to the front line, no more than two thousand yards away. He told me to get my driver. I did, and we rolled up our stuff. The colonel and his driver, and my driver and I, left and started back, not forward. Pretty soon we were joined by others- colonels and generals in their vehicles, and me, the ever-handy lieutenant. We drove all day long. We had no idea where we were going, but it was generally north. It turned out that we were the advance party for moving the Third Army to the rescue of the Battle of the Bulge. The Germans were running rampant. General Patton moved the Third Army almost overnight to go on the attack to block the Battle of the Bulge. This saved the country of Luxembourg from being invaded again by the Germans. Luxembourg City was one of the Germans' prime objectives, as was Antwerp and access to the English Channel.

We went on an all day long circuitous route. Finally, we stopped very late at night. General Patton was there, and my colonel got his orders. We then drove through the city of Luxembourg to a school house where we stopped. I unrolled my bedroll and got an hour's sleep. Suddenly, I felt someone kicking me. I opened one eye. It was my colonel. He told me to get up. I wanted to know why. He said he wouldn't tell me until I was wide awake. This was ominous. I woke up immediately and splashed some water on my face. He told me I was to go back through the city of Luxembourg that we'd just driven through the night before. I was to meet corps artillery and bring them to a town named Olingen which my colonel pointed out on the map. This was a lot to remember so I asked him for his map. He said he couldn't give it to me because it was the only one he had. He said he would give me a few minutes to look at it and make notes. I had a good driver, a

Tennessee boy, and I had him awake by then. He looked at the map with me and we made notes. When we went out of that place, it was snowing a blizzard. We couldn't see the roads. No vehicle had been over them. The only way we could tell what was a road was where there were fence lines or telephone poles on either side. Somehow or other, we found our way back through the city to the other side. We heard an enormous clanking noise. There came the Twelfth Corps Artillery. We slung the Jeep around and I said, "Follow me." We started back. When we got to the city of Luxembourg, the people were delirious to see this immense segment of the American Third Army clanking through the city to save them. They knew the Germans were on their way. As we continued through the city, I began to see the same cheering people that I had seen at first. I realized I was lost in the city with all this artillery following me. I came around a corner, and there was a six ton wrecker, an immense truck with a wrecker boom to pull tanks and things out of ditches. It had a sign on it which said "Last Vehicle Twelfth Corps Artillery." And I was the first vehicle, with twelve miles of artillery going through that city! And I was lost! It was pretty hilarious. Finally, finally, finally, I found someone who could tell me where the road was that I was looking for which would take us to Olingen. I got it all straightened out and we got there just in time to drop trails and start shooting. The Germans were literally coming over the hill.

Several years ago, I was honored by Luxembourg and the village of Olingen with a ceremony the likes of which you've never seen in your life. All of the people from Olingen were in a parade. They put on a banquet with wine by the barrelful. They had a band and the town fire truck, which was the only vehicle in the parade. Since all the people from the town were in the parade, the only ones left to watch it were the cows. It was exciting.

* * *

When we were in Germany on the attack, I had a German artillery shell hit in the backseat of my command car that killed everyone but me and the driver. The driver was wounded. I didn't get a scratch, but I had pieces of everybody all over me. The medics thought I was hit, too. But I said, "I'm all right, I'm all right." Somebody put a cigarette in my mouth. That was the only cigarette I ever smoked, and I didn't smoke it but a minute. I told them I wasn't hurt, and I wasn't.

One day I was in a Jeep, during an attack, and a sniper killed my driver. I was in the front passenger seat. The bullet had to have crossed right in front of me by only a few inches before it hit the driver in the heart.

Even after two such close calls, I was never so bold as to think I wouldn't be next. We didn't have much time to dwell upon what was going to happen to us today or tomorrow. My belief in the Lord was important. The 91st Psalm is potent stuff about having some divine protection. I felt that I had it.

I did what I had to do then. What terrifies me now, as an obvious elder, is wondering whether in this day and age, with the leadership we have now in Washington, D.C., we could ever again mount a dedicated army with the kind of people we have to deal with today. With the disregard for authority and discipline that is rampant in our schools and society in general, could we ever again take a citizen army and expect its members to listen to its officers? You have to have people who know how to obey an order. Insubordination cannot be tolerated.

The unit I fought the war with had been a National Guard unit out of the Detroit area. Most of the men were much older than me. I was only twenty-three years old. I was commanding men old enough to be my father. It was a very difficult thing. But we had discipline and that's what made us such a fearsome, fighting force. Our discipline was that we did what we had to do; what we were told to do.

* * *

One of my funniest encounters was when we crossed the Rhine. I was in a forward area while the engineers were building a bridge across the river at Oppenheim. This was where Julius Caesar crossed the Rhine River. It's one of the few places on that river where the current is impeded so that people can get across without a bridge. While the engineers were busy building the bridge, we were waiting so we could get more armor and artillery across. I was to get a communication line, a telephone line, across. General Patton came striding up to me with his pearl-handled pistols. He was a fearsome guy, about 6-foot 3-inches in height, a big man, but he had a squeaky voice. He started shouting at me to, "Do this, do that! Do this, do that!" It was at least sixteen things. I was just standing there, looking at him, and he wouldn't shut up, kept yelling at me. When he ran out of breath a little bit, I turned to him and he saw my cross cannons on my collar, which told him I was an artillery officer. Patton said, “Goddamn, you don’t have anything to do with those engineers, do you?” I answered him, “No, sir,” and saluted. That was my one and only one-on-one encounter with General George Patton. But I saw him very often, at least every week. He had a dog that went everywhere with him. He traveled everywhere in a Jeep that had a siren on the front of it. He made a lot of noise so everyone would get off the road and let him through. He was with the front line troops constantly, in evidence. He often came to the front and passed out decorations, medals to people, but then he was on his way out of there, quick!

This was General George Patton’s Christmas prayer, written in the chapel of Pescatore Foundation of the Grand Duchy of Luxembourg on December 23, 1944, of which a copy was given to every soldier:

“Lord, this is Patton speaking to you. These last two weeks were steps on our way to Hell. Rain, snow, more rain, and still more snow. I wonder, in vain, what’s going on in your headquarters? On which side do you really stand? For three years now, my chaplains have maintained this new war is a holy war, a new crusade, the only difference being that the soldiers of this age take cover in tanks. They claim that we crossed the Atlantic to decidedly defeat the German armies and their atheistic Fuehrer, and to restore peace and liberty in Europe. Until now I agreed with their statements because you gave us your complete support. A splendid sea and clear blue sky faciliated our landing in Africa and helped us to defeat Rommel. And the affair in Sicily was an expedition that didn’t amount to much. The weather was adequate for my tanks, and the accomplishment of what I would call the greatest victory you have granted to this day. You have guided me in the most grave decisions, even bringing the Germans into traps which facilitated my victory. But now, exactly at the halfway mark, you bet on another horse. It seems to me you put all your assets in Von Rundstedt’s hand, as he, let’s be honest, gives us much trouble. My army is not trained or conditioned to endure a winter campaign. And you know that this climate is much more convenient for Eskimos than for the Southern States Riders whom I command. Oh, Lord, after reading this weather forecast I’ve come to the conclusion that I may have offended you seriously, because I have to conclude that I’ve lost all your sympathy. It would be superfluous to add that our situation is now desperate. Of course I can go on telling my staff that all operations are developing as planned, but it is clear that my 101st Airborn

Division fighting in Bastogne is battling against the raging elements, and that Gaffey, one of my best generals, suffers much more from the climate than from the German attack. I am not in the habit of lamenting but my soldiers between Echternach and the Meuse are going through Hell. I visited some hospitals and I saw terrible things. But the most terrible of all is that the total absence of visibility keeps my airplanes stuck on the ground, thus my flying artillery without which I cannot fight, is useless. Even my reconnaissance planes cannot take off, and for fifteen days I haven't been able to find out what's going on behind the German lines. My God, it is impossible for me to fight in this gloom. Without your help, it will be impossible for me to study the enemy's tactics. Maybe you think I'm being unreasonable in talking to you, but I've lost all my patience with the chaplains who keep telling me that this atmospheric situation is typical Ardennes climate. To Hell with faith and patience! You have to make up your mind now. You have to help me so that on the occasion of your Son's birthday, I can offer Him the whole German army as a Christmas present. Lord, I'm not unreasonable. I don't ask for impossible things. I don't want to perform a miracle. All I'm asking for is four days of clear weather. Consent to give me as your gift four days of blue skies so that my airplanes can take off, hunt, bomb, find their goals and annihilate them. Give me four days so that this mud can harden, allow my trucks to roll along and supply provisions and ammunition to my infantry which needs it urgently. I need four whole days in order to send Von Rundstedt and his army into the middle of Valhalla. It is too much of a burden for me to stand by powerless at this needless holocaust of our American youth. Amen."

The next day, Christmas Day, dawned bright and sunny. By noon, every airplane that could fly was in the air. I know because I was there.

* * *

Corporal Cwicklowski was a fine motor mechanic. He could keep every Jeep, halftrack, and truck we had in running condition, not an easy job when you consider most were constantly being shot full of holes. That's why we hated to lose him when we were charging across France in August of 1944. He knew all about welding, tuning carburetors, and changing tank tracks, but nothing at all about the finer points of consuming French liquor. In fact, this Polish American G.I. from Hamtramck, Michigan, didn't know a damn thing about wine, cognac, B & B, or Calvados. It was all just alcohol to him and he could drink a barrel of it. That's how we nearly lost him for good. After a particularly intense counter attack by an armored division or two, we found Corportal "Cwick" among those missing in action. He wasn't the kind to desert, but no one had seen him get hit, and his remains were not to be found. Since all of our vehicles had suffered damage, it was imperative that the motor section get busy at once. My Jeep looked like a sieve. I hadn't been in it. And the colonel's command car looked real bad, too. That's when we mounted a search at the field hospital and graves registration unit. About this time, a young Frenchman gave us a clue. "Look in the village," the interpreter translated. I was ordered to find him fast. With two enlisted men, and our Free French guide, we set out in a semi-attack weapons carrier. The trail lead to a roofless and smoldering barn. Only the roof had been shot away. There we found our missing corporal. He and a French farmer were lying on the floor, flat on their backs, their mouths wide open beneath the spigot of a freshly distilled batch of Calvados.

"Cwick" was still alive, but barely. So, we did the only sensible thing under the circumstances. We tossed him into the back of an ammunition truck and let him sober up. We hauled him around for a week before he was fit for duty. A good mechanic was too valuable to evacuate to the field hospital. We would have never seen him again if the medics had gotten hold of him.

* * *

We were fighting in eastern France near Nancy in the fall of 1944 when General Patton's Third Army ran out of gas. The Germans quickly sensed our situation and stepped up their incessant artillery attack. Nightly we were shelled for hours and we were losing men and vehicles at an alarming rate. It was decided to move the command post to the comparative safety of a secluded farm near the village of Athienville. The day we set up position was cold and dreary. Bunking in a barn full of mice was not too thrilling either. Then the G.I.s made a startling discovery- the farmer, who was none too friendly, spoke only German. And he kicked his dog; very repulsive to our men. But his barn was full of food. Most of it was very much the live variety, on two to four legs, and all quite edible. In addition, there was a cellar stocked with potatoes, onions, cabbages, and wine. Since we'd been on "K" and "C" rations for a period of three months, what could be wrong with some fried chicken and a few fried onions and potatoes, with a bit of Moselle to wash it down? Next went all the ducks and rabbits, followed by a wild boar shot by one of our soldiers. After two weeks, there was nothing left. Almost every pig, pickle, and pullet had been eaten. Almost. During our sojourn on the farm, someone noticed that the farmer, who by now was even less friendly, pulled a chain each night which let the water out of a small pond. The escaping water turned a tiny generator. We'd have electricity until he pulled it a second time and shut it off and went to bed. One morning I awakened to the shouts of fifty G.I.s. They had drained the pond and were hip deep in mud catching the fish with their bare hands. That was really the end of the food. A few days later we moved forward to Morhange where the accommodations were not so nice and the fighting was more intense. The infantry and tanks slugged it out for weeks and couldn't advance a mile. Suddenly, General Patton had a brilliant idea.

Why not disengage Fourth Armored, go to the rear, rest and regroup, then hit the line in another place? I was part of the reconnaissance team charged with the responsibility of selecting the new position well to the rear. As Colonel Gray and I drove down the road, things began to look very familiar. We were right back at our favorite farm near Athienville. The colonel looked at me and said, "Why not?" An hour later we moved into the same position we had left a month before. I can still see the sad look on that farmer's face. This time I issued an order: Hands off, or else! We stayed only a couple of days this time, and when we left to go back into battle, our mess sergeant provided the farmer with enough food to get his family through the winter. And all of his new chickens were left intact. So, with the fresh egg the farmer gave me as he wished me good luck I was to need, we again went out to the attack.

A few years ago, we were driving through France, near Athienville, and I thought I could find that farm, but I didn't try. There were too many horrible memories of the battle near there.

* * *

Not all of my war stories have had happy endings, but this one does. It's happy from start to finish. Joe Andrews and I were the closest of boyhood friends. Our fathers were close friends, too. Joe and I literally had grown up together. It was a wonderful surprise when I walked into the command post late one night to hear Colonel Guthrie saying, " Do you understand this fire control mission, Lieutenant Andrews?" I looked up from the warm stove to see my friend, Joe. We'd just been joined by the Twenty-sixth Infantry Division, fresh from the states. Joe was the new liaison officer attached to our unit. This was his first night in the combat area. We were bogged down in the Seigfried Line, so it was comforting to have some infantry out in front of us for a change. After Joe had completed his duties, we had time for a wonderful visit. We talked all night. As I remember, he had seen my wife at church only a few weeks previous. All the news from home was good to hear. We would be together for an indefinite period. The very next morning, Joe and I were standing a foot apart in the kitchen of a small house that I was using as a communications center, when all hell broke loose. Two 88 shells hit in the road in front of the house. A second later, two more slammed into the house. The dust and smell of explosives were overpowering. As he grabbed his leg, Joe began to yell, "I'm hit! I'm hit!" I looked to see if I could help him, only to discover that a fragment from the exploding shell had gone through his canteen, and water was gushing out of both sides and pouring down his trousers. "You're not hit, that's just water," I said. "No, look at my pants. Only it doesn't hurt," he shouted. By then I was laughing so hard, I was crying. Joe was so mad at me for laughing he was ready to shoot me. We were together for the next two or three weeks during some of the most intense and difficult fighting of the entire war, giving each other much needed moral support. Eventually, we no longer needed the fire support of the Twenty-sixth Infantry, and we separated, not to see each other until after we got home from the war, both of us without a scratch.

* * *

I have been blessed. When I was in school, my teachers were wonderful, wonderful people. I received a marvelous education in junior high and at Classen High School, particularly in language. I remember my teachers and their names like it was yesterday. My debate team even won the national championship. The teachers took an interest in the students and were our role models; our heroes.

I was a very successful merchant. My father and I were in business together and my parents were retailers in Oklahoma City for many years.

Robert Orbach

Probably, I would change something about my life, if I could, but that's only to say that perhaps I would rather have been something like a college professor with an independent income rather than a clothing merchant. I think teaching is something I would have been good at and enjoyed, although I have enjoyed everything I have ever done.

My best advice to someone just starting out is to always tell the truth because that way one doesn't have to try to remember what was said. Remember that the truth takes time, it's not always quickly and easily told. Truth solves all problems and lasts forever.

CHAPTER FIFTEEN

MERLE FRANCIS PETERSON

JULY 29, 1998

My family was from Jonesboro, Arkansas. I moved down to Dumas, Arkansas, in April 1939. I got into the Ford business on November 1, 1939; then got married on November 19, 1939. When I left for the service, there were no cars to sell. All the factories were shut down during World War II. I left the dealership in my wife's hands. She kept it going by running the repair service.

I was twenty-six years old when I started out as a cadet in 1942. I was commissioned and was going to fly with the air corps, but I couldn't pass my flight physical because of my eyes, so I had to take to the ground. With my engineering education, I ended up as a ground officer in the air corps.

I went to Columbia, South Carolina to get my armament and was with the B-25 armor outfit. From there, I went to Walterboro, South Carolina and trained with an outfit. Then we prepared to go overseas. I was in the 340th Bomb Group, 489th Bomb Squadron.

We went to Suez, Egypt and traveled across the desert where we were in combat in North Africa, Tunisia. This was during General Montgomery's time when he was chasing Rommel. After we got Rommel off North Africa, we went to Sicily; then through Italy to the island of Corsica where we spent a year.

The main job of my group was to load the bombs and ammunition onto the B-25 planes. The bombs were loaded onto the planes and hung up in the bomb bay. The bombs had a fuse which had a wire to it and when the bombs were armed, the fuse would hang down in the bomb bay. This allowed the bomb to explode when it hit. We carried 100-pound bombs, 500-pound bombs, and a couple of 1000-pound bombs. We could hang the 100-pounders by hand, muscle them up.

One of the interesting things about being in the service was meeting men from all over the United States who had come together. I remember some of them in our outfit who were from New Jersey and talked a little different from us Arkansans. Referring to some men who were on strike, one of the New Jersey men who drove an oil (erl) truck said, “They ought to berl them in erl.”

Another time, when we were in Sicily, some of the Italian Americans in our outfit saw a Sicilian man with a two-wheel cart drawn by a donkey. These boys couldn’t wait to try out their own Italian language. One of the Americans tried to communicate with the Sicilian in Italian, only to find out that he was an American from Omaha, Nebraska, who’d gotten caught over there when the war started. He was so happy to see us.

An exciting thing happened while we were in Italy. We were at Pompei, under the volcano, Vesuvius, when it erupted in 1943. It knocked out eighty-four of our planes. There were about eighteen inches of ash. The sediment covered everything. All the cloth parts of our planes were ripped up.

One of our crews was sent to bomb a railway. After the bombs were dropped, pictures were taken to confirm their mission. When the crew got back they reported that they’d bombed the fool out of them, but the pictures told a different story. In fact, they’d missed the target and gone over and hit a graveyard. One of the old sergeants said, “Well, there’s nothing like making sure.” Things like that went on all the time, so we were aptly entertained.

We lost many planes. It was bad when somebody was just getting through with his missions and getting ready to go home, then he got shot down and lost his life. Our pilots were supposed to fly fifty missions. If a pilot flew everyday, he might get his missions done in less than two months. The average time was six or seven months.

I had some close shaves, but then I have that just driving out on the highway. One night in Corsica we got bombed, and I didn’t have a slit trench. All I could do was lie on my bed and pray they wouldn’t hit me. Shrapnel went through the top of my tent and twenty feet behind the tent. Men who had slit trenches, and were in them, got killed when the explosives rolled into where they were. And that was only twenty feet behind my tent! Sometimes I had to think the good Lord was taking care of me. It made me think because I was spared there was special purpose to my life, and that I'd better get home and get with it. I matured a lot.

I got a good lesson from being in the service. It was that people don't realize how good they have it back here in the States. It made me think; made me appreciate my country. It was a good experience. Patriotism is serving your country in any way that you can. Some can do better at one thing than another. I didn't know what I could do, but I did what they asked me to do. I don't feel like I sacrificed too much because there were a million others in the same shoes.

After I got out of the service, I was on recreation leave. I got on a soft bed in one of the hotels and couldn't sleep. Put me back on a hard cot, and I could sleep away, but on that soft bed, I couldn't sleep at all.

I came back home in June 1945. We didn't get any cars to sell until 1946. It was four years that there were no cars or trucks being made to sell. All the transportation had been worn out. I retired from the automobile business when I was sixty years old. I said it was a young man's game. Then I got into other things. It's important to keep my mind and body busy. I'm never going to completely retire. I'll have to be carried out.

Being in the war may have given me a different outlook on world things. It took me around the world, and I've been every place since then. If not for the war, and seeing some of the world, I wouldn't have been as interested in traveling to see the rest of it.

When I got out of college in 1938, I couldn't get a job. The first job I got was running a service station. I made ten dollars a week. There was a boy who went to school with me. He copied everything I wrote down. His daddy knew a United States Senator, and that got him a big job with the Work Progress Administration. I said to myself right then, it isn't what you know, it's who you know. You can always find somebody who will help you. I'll tell you this: I'll help someone get a job, but I won't help him keep it.

Although my wife and I have never had any children of our own, we've adopted everybody else's children. I support ten scholarships at the University of Arkansas at Monticello. It will pay half a student's tuition. And those students will make it with just a little help. It might be for a high school student, or maybe a single mother trying to get an education to support her family. They can't make a living without an education. It's one of the ways I keep going. I appreciate what the good Lord's granted me and I'm not going to take it with me. I'm going to do what I can just as long as I'm here. That's the reason I try to do as many things for the community as I can, and I want to continue.

The only thing I want people to remember me for is that "I did what I said I'd do." I want my word to be as good as gold. I don't need a contract; a handshake will do. I want to be remembered as doing something to improve our town. I believe in education and that's why I spend money on schools.

Things were different when we were growing up. Our morals were higher. I think television and reading materials have been the main influences on today's younger generations. The best thing is a good family life at home. You need two parents to put their fingers on things and say when you can't do something. I remember back years ago when it came out that kids should be allowed to express themselves, just let them do anything they want to. That's when things went to hell right quick. Everybody needs guidance. Something that worries me is marriage in today's society. People divorce too easily.

What I'd tell young folks is that if they're willing to put out, to work hard, they can do anything they want to do. One thing I'd like to get across is that anybody can be a millionaire if you're willing to do without the little things you might spend your money for. Do by doing without. You've got to spend less than you make; make investments, and reinvestments. Don't throw away money you can use for a good cause. Then you'll realize the enjoyment.

I've tried to tell young folks to take care of themselves. I'm now eighty-two years old, and I've taken care of myself all my life. I never did smoke or drink or anything like that. It was there for me, but I'd give it to someone else who wanted it. That gave me less to overcome. Many of my compatriots are no longer with us.

I've had a wonderful life. I wouldn't change any part of it. I feel good about what I do. I try to keep everything right on top of the table. And I'm a hugger- it's much better than an old cold handshake. I'm just the way I am: I love people. And I'll do anything I can to help people. I'm a giver, not a taker.

Merle Francis Peterson

I felt like I owed some service, so in 1960 I ran for the Arkansas State Senate, and I won. When I went into the legislature, I told Governor Faubus, "If I ask for anything, turn me down. But if I ask for something for my people, you'd better listen to me." He and I were real close friends until he died.

I like to think my life's been an open book, and I'd like to keep it open as long as I can. There are just so many things that need to be done, and I want to be around doing them.

CHAPTER SIXTEEN

OTTO RAHILL

DECEMBER 2, 1998

Few homes had four-star flags in their windows, but my parents' home did. This was during World War II when all four of their sons were serving at the same time. In June 1944, my mother, Lillie Rahill, was pictured on the front page of the Oklahoma City newspaper staring out her window where this flag was displayed, contemplating the absence of her sons. It was a hard time for our family.

First, oldest brother Roy volunteered and went to war. Then the youngest, Mike, was drafted. Following shortly, was second oldest, myself, who enlisted. Then Arthur "Fuzzy" finally got over there. Roy was in France, Mike was in the Pacific, I was in North Africa and Italy, and Fuzzy was in England. The only one left at home with my parents was one of my sisters. It was tough on them. They didn't know what we were going to get into.

* * *

On December 7, 1941, a Sunday afternoon, I'd gone to the drug store. I heard about the attack on Pearl Harbor while there. I went running home to find everyone gathered in front of our Zenith radio. My mother was crying up a storm, knowing that all her sons were of age to go to war.

My family was going to need some extra money, so my brother, Fuzzy, and I decided to go to machine shop school at night. Since 1939, after graduating from high school, I worked a full-time job during the day at Harbor and Longmeyer Furniture Store as an elevator operator. I earned twenty-five cents an hour. I would eat and rest a while after working at the furniture store, then at 11:30 that night, go to machine shop school until 7:30 the next morning, then go home and get cleaned up and go straight to work at the furniture store. One time I fell asleep running a lathe. That'll wake you up in a hurry, I'll guarantee you. What tuppence I had, I used to help support my family. I kept two dollars each pay day. That would last me a couple of weeks. Two dollars went a long ways back then.

Then I had the opportunity to go to Saint Louis to work for the government. I had never left home before. It wasn't easy to go, but I did. I was about twenty years old.

In Saint Louis, I was placed at Emerson Electric as a government inspector. I was in charge of a large number of women performing inspections in mass production. They were all smokers. I had to fish them out of the restroom from smoking cigarettes to get them back on the job. I knocked on the door, but they wouldn't come out, so I had to go in and get them. We were making nose fuses, M-20 boosters up to 75mm to go in a 155 howitzer shell. So many thousand per minute were supposed to be inspected, and the work piled up while the ladies sat smoking. I worked there for a year.

When I heard that my youngest brother, Mike, was drafted into service right out of high school, I left Saint Louis and returned home to Oklahoma City. I went to the draft board and enlisted. If my brother had to go, then I would, too.

I was told I would be attached to the air force as ordnance, a bomb-handler. I left home again on January 15, 1943. I spent one week at Fort Sill, Oklahoma, in boot camp. My uniform didn't fit me, and I couldn't do an about-face, in fact, I still can't. Then we were taken by train to Jefferson Barracks, Missouri, right outside Saint Louis. We were at Jefferson Barracks at the time when a large number of men there died during a pneumonia outbreak.

From Jefferson Barracks, we headed by train to California to an ordnance school. While we were on the train we were fed soup and coffee from big galvanized garbage cans. They put a two-by-four board in them to keep it from splashing. We lined up by the hundreds to eat, returning to our seats with our plates and canteens. When we got to California, they bunked us at the Santa Anita Race Track where the horses were evacuated. We slept in the stables on cots. It wasn't that bad really. Those horses had it pretty good there at Santa Anita.

The first day we went to class we were told that we would be overseas by the end of June, and it came true. After thirty days, we left California and rode on a train to New York. They kept the shades pulled down. We were not allowed to look out as we traveled across the country because they didn't want people to know there were troops on the train. We left Camp Pines, New York, arriving June 29 at three o'clock in the afternoon in Oran, North Africa. They strapped a full field pack on our shoulders, with an M-1 rifle, and we stayed on the ship with all our gear until the wee hours of the morning. Then they unloaded us into trucks. They stood us in there, so many and so close, that we couldn't have fallen over. We were like cattle. We still had on our field packs and we were exhausted. They drove us to a camp area where there were rows of six-men tents. The truck would pull up to a tent, and we were told, "Okay, six of you fall out." It continued like that down the row of tents. When I got out, about midway down the row, I was pooped. I unshackled my field pack and got over in a corner and fell asleep across it. When I woke up, I was sore and stiff from carrying that field pack and rifle for so long. I was dog-tired. The next morning, they gave us a fifteen-pound sledge hammer and said to go break rock. This was to build a runway for the airplanes. This went on for a week or so.

I was in the Fifteenth Air Force, 97th Bomb Group, 414th Bomb Squadron. I was the crew chief for the bomb-handling crew. We loaded the bombs on the B-17 airplanes. From Oran, North Africa, we went to Algiers on our way to Tunisia.

While in Algiers, there was a rain storm you wouldn't believe. We weren't protected in our trucks because they were open. We had to spend the night there, so I climbed up on a hill and put a piece of tent down on the ground. I put it on a slope where the water would run around it, and I covered up with a piece of tent, then lay down on the side of the mountain and went to sleep with the rain pounding down on me. Next morning, we moved on up a little farther and made it to Tunisia. We went to Sicily, and from there, we went to Foggia in southern Italy. We were bringing up the rear, and when we got to Italy, we were close enough to the front line to see the flashes on the artillery. That was pretty darn close for our B-17s.

By this time, I had grown a beard. Another soldier who was a friend from Oklahoma City, Cecil Saied, saw my name on a bulletin board and came to look me up while I was in Foggia. When he found me in the camp, we were sitting in the tent watching a candle burn for entertainment, and I had my feet propped up on a table, drinking a beer. He didn't even recognize me with the beard. Cecil told that story until the day he died, that he went to see me and didn't even know me.

In Foggia, I'll tell you, it was bad. The bomb dumps were five miles from camp. The bombs came over on transport planes and ships, and were left on the dirt, which was fine until it rained. The bombs would get buried in the mud and we had to hook a boom on them, and pull them out of the mud with a truck. We loaded them onto trailers, then hauled them to the planes, three or four miles away. We had 100-pound bombs, 500-pound bombs, 1000-pound bombs, fragmentation bombs, and incendiary bombs. I weighed about one hundred twenty-four pounds at the time. With a bomb hook, I could carry two 100-pound bombs at the same time, one in each hand. We hand-loaded those 100-pounders, and the cluster bombs. One time I was loading a 250-pound bomb and the fin came loose. The bomb twisted on me, and I dropped it. It fell, hitting me right in the stomach, knocking me down and out. I lost consciousness, but I was all right. I got up and finished the job. Another time, we were at the bomb dump loading bombs on the trailer. I was down hooking the hoist to one of the bombs. As my hand was on one of the back plates, another bomb slammed into that one, catching my hand between two 500-pound bombs. It crushed two fingers on my left hand. Then we had five miles of bad roads to get back to the dispensary. I was laid up for a while. After the bones healed and my fingers were out of the cast, the sergeant would forcefully bend my fingers to get them back in shape. I would scream my head off, but he'd bend them anyway. After I got back out to work, just using my hand as we loaded the bombs got it back in shape. In every picture I sent home to my mother, I was hiding that bandaged hand behind me. Although I never told her about getting hurt, the first thing she did after I got back home was to grab that hand and check it out. Mothers just have a way of knowing those kinds of things.

We used to arm the bombs by putting in both the tail fuse and the nose fuse before loading the them on the trailer. Then we'd transport them to the planes and put them up in the bomb bay. We would back up a trailer with twelve 500-pound armed bombs on it to the plane. The nose fuse armed itself by centrifugal force, but the tail fuse could arm itself by impact. When the bomb hit the ground, if the nose fuse didn't ignite or explode it, the tail fuse would. It was a back-up fuse. We had to quit doing it that way because of what happened...

One evening, as one of the crews was loading the armed bombs on a plane, one of the bombs fell out of the hoist, hit the trailer and exploded. It blew up that airplane and another one, and tore up four more, as twenty-four bombs went off. It knocked a hole in the ground as big as a house. The gas tanks on the planes were full, and all the machine guns were loaded with ammunition. When the explosions began, bullets began firing everywhere. Six men were killed.

I was supposed to be loading bombs on one of those planes that blew up, but I was sent on an errand. When I came back, another crew had taken over that plane, and I began helping on another one. I was putting on a tail fuse, and the tail fin was laying flat on the ground between my feet, when the bombs and planes exploded, and bullets began flying. So help me, a 50-caliber bullet went right through that tail fin between my feet! It just missed me.

We ran and ran through the dark, seeing parts of airplanes on fire everywhere, raining down around us. We ran to our foxholes which were almost two miles away. Our foxhole was right behind our tent. I fell into it, exhausted from running. Later we saw where a bomb plate had gone through a rack of clothes in our tent, and out the other side. That bomb plate must have blown right over our heads as we were in the foxhole. We were called together for a roll call. They told us we didn't have to go back out there if we didn't want to, but we decided we might as well keep at it. We didn't let them replace us. From that day forward, we never put a fuse in a bomb until it was loaded into the airplane.

* * *

My mother sent all kinds of things, like cigarettes and letters. But one time she sent fried chicken. She sent it to each of her four sons in different places, and this is how she did it:

She fried the chicken and put it in a large glass container, pouring the grease back over it to preserve it. Then she sealed it with canning wax, and baked the whole thing in a big loaf of bread. When it arrived after thirty days, the bread was as hard as could be. We broke it off and found the fried chicken in perfect condition. All we had to do was heat it up. It tasted like she'd just cooked it. It smelled so good! Everybody wanted a piece of that chicken, so as it turned out, I got only one piece for myself.

We used to make coffee outside behind the tent. We made it in a can. When the water boiled, we'd put in the coffee. One time, the last of our coffee became infested with ants. It was all the coffee we had, so we used it anyway. We put in the coffee, ants, and everything, and cooked it till it was almost like candy, and drank it anyway. It was the strongest coffee I ever drank in my life...ants and all.

We had a mattress sack we filled with straw and wrapped in a blanket. This was on our cot. And we'd put a mosquito net up around our bed at night, strung up between poles at each end. I was all tucked in one night, and just falling asleep, when I felt something crawl across my face. It was a mouse. How I got out of that tent I'll never know, because I was so tucked in. The next day we dug up our tent's wood floor and found a whole nest of mice underground. We took care of those mice. The next night I slept better.

We played poker a lot. The men and officers played together. I lost all the money I had in a twenty-five cent poker game. And I missed a promotion because of what I said to a kibitzing lieutenant. I ran him out of the tent after telling him to either sit down and play cards, or stand there and watch with his mouth shut. When the promotions came out, I should have been made a corporal or a sergeant, but that lieutenant kept me from it.

* * *

After the war was over, the plan was to ship us over to the South Pacific by way of the United States. I had been in the service almost three years without any type of leave, not even a three-day pass, so as I was waiting to be shipped, I applied for a rest leave. The Red Cross located my brother, Fuzzy, who was over in England in the service.

Fuzzy was the adventurous type who wanted to see the world. But he had quite a time getting out of Oklahoma. At first he was sent to Enid, Oklahoma, and he hitch-hiked home every weekend. He kept asking for a transfer. Finally, he got his transfer...to Tinker Air Force Base, right back in Oklahoma City, where he got to go home every night. He thought he would never get out of Oklahoma! Next he was sent to Will Rogers World Airport, still in his hometown! He finally got to England in the Quartermaster Corps. While there, an elementary school was bombed, and Fuzzy helped carry out all the little children who were injured. He went back to England twice after the war to see people whom he had befriended while in the service there. They never lost touch after all those years.

I went to London to see Fuzzy on my leave. We had four days together. I ate fish and chips, and drank too much ale. And Fuzzy was just his usual self, speaking to every pretty girl on the street, giving each one a hug and a kiss. He could always get by with that kind of thing. We rented a Volkswagen cab with an open top that we could stand and look out. We paid the cab driver five dollars in English money to take us all around. And we had a camera. We took a picture of every pretty girl in London. Those girls would stop and smile so sweet. It seemed we must have taken a thousand pictures. At the end, we discovered there wasn't a bit of film in that camera. Fuzzy said that he had to hold me up by the heels and let the beer run out of me, because I got sick from drinking too much.

We were in Piccadilly Circus on V-J Day. There were thousands of people gathered around when we heard the news that the war in Japan was over. Everybody was so happy. At that time, we didn't know it, but our youngest brother, Mike, was on a ship headed to Tokyo. I returned to Italy after four days, and left for the United States on September 15, 1945.

I couldn't wait to get back home to Oklahoma. After being away for three years, I surprised my mother at the front door. We hadn't seen each other since the day I left for the war. I rang the doorbell, and when she saw it was me, she went to pieces. And so did I. Looking back, I should have called and let her know I was coming. That was fifty-three years ago.

* * *

This is God's country, no question about it. A working man in this country can have the best of everything. That's worth something. A soldier in any branch of the United States military is the best there is, and has it better than any other soldier in the world. If you want to live in a country like ours, you have to have loyalty towards it, and this defines patriotism. As my brother, Roy, said, "It's the ones who didn't come back from the war who were the real heroes."

Otto Rahill

Sometimes someone has to do the dirty work, and my generation had to go do part of it. I think it was worth it. If I had it to do all over again, I wouldn't change much. I was scared when I was in the war, and I prayed every night. When we heard the sound of an air raid alert, we'd run for the foxhole, and we were scared. But I got through it.

My advice to others is to be honest and kind to your fellow man. Treat others with respect and don't be too prejudiced. And get educated. The only thing I wish I could do over is my education. I grew up during The Depression and it was tough. I worked before school and after school. The daily thirty cents I made went to help our family buy food to eat. At times, I was just too tired from working to concentrate on schoolwork. I remember sleeping during Spanish class. It was the only bad grade I ever made. When I got back from the war, I attended college on the G. I. Bill and studied accounting, but I stopped just short of getting my degree. And that's the only thing I wish I could do differently- complete my education.

I have most loved my family, my church, and God, and friends. A man without a friend is pretty lonely, you know that? People will probably remember me as a friendly, nice guy; someone who was pleasant, and a God-fearing man. Every night when I go to bed, I say The Lord's Prayer, and I thank God for all His blessings. I pray that He will continue to bless me so that I may share it with my fellow man. That's how I live my life, and that's what I do.

Chapter Seventeen

Glenn H. Rojohn

December 19, 1998

I was born in Greenock, Pennsylvania, on April 6, 1922. It was a German community. I was born there, I've always lived there, and I tell people the only way I'll ever get out of Greenock is feet first.

In 1942, I was about to be drafted. A man named Ray Bowman who worked at my dad's Buick dealership recommended I join the air force. I had never been in an airplane before, but in September I went down and enlisted. First I went to Fort Mead in New Jersey for processing, and was sent back home to do recruitment duty from September 1942 until the early part of 1943. I was then shipped to Nashville, Tennessee, for cadet processing. My younger brother, Leonard, unbeknownst to me, enlisted in the air force, and by coincidence, we both ended up in Nashville at the same time.

My brother and I were in the same cadet class, the same barracks, and we had the same instructors all the way though preflight training. I told our commanding officer I thought this wasn't a good idea. But we were both sent to Stuttgart, Arkansas. I remember on New Year's Eve 1943, Leonard and I flew around and around together over Little Rock, Arkansas, to get in our flying hours. We graduated in January 7, 1944, as second lieutenants.

We went to Chanute Field near Chicago for B-17 training; then Fort Worth where we soloed the B-17 together. Until then we had always had an instructor with us. We took turns as pilot and co-pilot, with a flight engineer present. After that, we went to Salt Lake City where we picked up our B-17 crews, and on to Dalhart, Texas, where we became acquainted with our crews and trained with them. From there, we went to Gulfport, Mississippi; and last stop was Langley Field in Virginia for radar training. By now it was the middle of the summer in 1944.

I got my orders to fly overseas. Leonard was sick with tonsillitis and didn't go at the same time. After I was assigned to my bomb group, I never knew what became of my brother. After I was overseas, I had a pass and went into London. Who did I run into on the street, but Leonard? What were the odds of that happening? It was such a coincidence. That's when we exchanged information about which groups we were in. I was in the Bloody Hundredth, 349th Squadron.

In December 1944, after flying several missions in a row, I was scheduled to go on a leave, but we were put on maximum effort and my pass was canceled. This was my twenty-second mission and it was to Hamburg, Germany. Thirty-seven bombers took off from Thorpe Abbotts, England, on December 31, but only twenty-five returned.

After bombing our target, we were returning to base when we got into a tremendous German fighter attack over the North Sea. Our formation was riddled, and we lost ten planes just like that. I was trying to fill a void in the formation to keep it intact. All of a sudden, I heard a crash and didn't know what was going on. Then I realized that our plane was stuck together with another bomber. The co-pilot and I did everything we could think of to try and separate the two, but we couldn't. We were on fire, and the bottom plane was on fire. Our engines were still running, so I shut them down to try to control the fire. Three of the other plane's engines were still running. The way the two planes stuck together were that the guns on the top turret of the lower plane came up through the belly of my plane, and then the tails locked together. It was a perfect match. Our lower ball turret gunner, Joseph Russo, didn't have a chance.

We were able to maintain the plane so that the other crew members could bail out. The ball turret gunner, navigator, bombardier, and one waist gunner survived from the bottom plane. They had bailed out right away. The navigator from the bottom ship claimed that his pilot and co-pilot were mortally wounded in the fighter attack causing them to lose control of their plane. Two of my crew bailed out too quick and drowned in the ocean. This was one of the waist gunners and the tail gunner. This was not my original tail gunner, Herman Horencamp, who had flown all my other missions with me. He had gotten frostbite on his ears and didn't make this mission. He was so worked up over what happened to his crew, that he never flew another mission after that.

I was sure I was going to die. I had always been a religious person, and the only thing I really remember doing is reciting the Lord's Prayer on the way down. The only escape hatch available was back by the tail. For me to let go of the controls and try to get to that door was an impossibility, for as soon as I would have let go, the plane would have gone into a spiral spin and the force would have pinned me down. I felt that I could hold the planes together, and I ordered my co-pilot, William Leek, to bail, but he refused my order. His refusal was what saved my life, because it took both of us to hold the planes together before we crash landed over Germany. When we hit the ground, my plane slid off the other one and went another hundred yards or so. The bottom plane exploded. Russo, in the lower ball turret, must have died on impact.

Our plane was pretty well mashed up, but we were able to get out on the wing. The first thing Bill Leek did was to reach into his pocket for a cigarette. But a German was right there and knocked it out of his hand, saying, "For you, the war is over." Bill had been standing on a gasoline-soaked wing, and if he had lit that cigarette, we would have gone up in an explosion. They captured us immediately, for they had watched us come down.

I was in solitary confinement for a number of days at a German headquarters near Frankfurt. They were trying to soften me up, but I never told anything but my name, rank, and serial number. When finally I was questioned by a German captain, unbelievably, he was very well informed. He told me everything that had happened at my base since I left. They had a dossier on me and knew where I had worked, where I went to high school, that I was on the tennis team, even what my dad did for a living. Evidently, their intelligence and spies had found out most of this from newspaper accounts in my hometown. So, I told that captain there wasn't anything I could tell him that he didn't already know. I was taken to the prison camp Stalag I on the Baltic Sea, near Poland. The Russians liberated us out of there in May 1945. Fortunately, the Geneva Convention stated that prisoners of war were not to be mistreated, so my five months as a prisoner at the end of the war was not nearly as bad as some other prisoners suffered. I was not mistreated, except for not having anything to eat. Of course, at the tail end of the war, the Germans didn't have anything to eat either.

During the last two months we occasionally had ersatz bread which contained sawdust, each loaf weighing about twelve pounds, and we had rutabagas boiled with no seasoning, just plain rutabagas.

I was married in February 1946. The young preacher who married us asked me if there was anything special I wanted in our vows. I said, "Yeah, if I ever come up the driveway and smell rutabagas cooking, this marriage is gone." My wife has never cooked a rutabaga!

On that New Year's Eve in 1944, my brother, Leonard, just happened to call the base to find out if I was going on a leave, only to find out that I was shot down with no more information than that. Then my brother got some time off and tried to find out from witnesses what had happened that day. He wrote home to our mother to try to explain to her what had transpired. She got Leonard's letter before the telegram telling her I was missing in action. It wasn't until March that my parents knew I was in a prison camp. I was permitted to send a radiogram from the prison interrogation center. Several ham radio operators on the east coast picked this up and sent a note to my parents telling them I was alive. Our being in the war affected my mother tremendously, she lost every bit of hair on her body. She became completely bald due to the stress. I felt so bad about it.

I grew up in a religious family and lived my childhood by The Golden Rule. I have continued to live by my religious beliefs. Every New Year's Eve, the anniversary of my crash in Germany, for the last fifty-four years I've gone to church first and then partied after.

* * *

For years, I refused to tell this story, although I had opportunities to do so. I turned down NBC for a documentary because I didn't know where my co-pilot, Bill Leek, was or what had happened to him. After more than forty years, I found Bill by answering an ad in a magazine which claimed to be able to find anybody. About ten days later, I got a note back with a telephone number to try. When the woman answered the phone, I asked if this was the Leek residence. She said, "Yes." And I asked if Bill was there. She said, "Yes, do you want to talk to him?" Bill lived out in California, but was there

Glenn H. Rojohn

in Washington that day visiting his mother whose number I had called. We had a very emotional time on the telephone.

This was in 1987, and later that year in October, the 100th Bomb Group reunion was held in Long Beach, California, where Bill and I planned to meet. After getting there, I was making an inquiry about where to find him, when Bill and his wife approached us. We knew each other immediately and it was quite emotional. Five of my crew were at that particular reunion. Bill and I spent several days together during that time, and we cried as we parted.

In April 1988, I got a phone call that Bill died during a stress test... just months after our only reunion.

* * *

In 1996, I returned to Germany to the little town called Tettens near where our planes crashed. The witnesses there said that I turned the plane just in time to miss their town, but I don't remember that. Some people now have tried to portray me as a hero for what we went through in the war, but I don't want any part of that, because I don't think I am one. I'd like to be remembered, not as a hero, but as a man who fought for my country.

As I've spoken to high school assemblies, I am amazed at the questions the students ask. These kids are very attentive and hungry for information about World War II. That's why I think this generation is coming around in a positive way, a patriotic way. When I first enlisted, I didn't feel particularly patriotic. A feeling of purpose and patriotism kicked in when I realized I was there to defend my country. I was there to do a job. We have to do everything that's possible to be able to be a free country. We can't allow any aggression. We need to be a free world, really. What it takes to do that is for people to love their country and their freedom.

Chapter Eighteen

Leonard E. Rojohn

December 19, 1998

I was born on the couch in my family's living room on March 8, 1925, in Greenock, Pennsylvania. The doctor came to our home for the birth. I was raised in Greenock and went to school there. In high school, I took mostly commercial courses, never thinking I would go to college because our family was still recovering from the Great Depression. My typing teacher's brother was in charge of air force recruiting in Pittsburgh. As I approached my eighteenth birthday and draft age, my teacher suggested the air force for me so I wouldn't be living in trenches for the next three years. That's how I got into the air force. I was still in high school when I enlisted and left for Nashville, Tennessee. I got my high school diploma after returning home from the war.

At my parents' home, we had a pool table in the basement. My mother and I used to shoot pool together. Telling this story is really the only time I get emotional. When I left, she said, "Let's go downstairs and have one last pool game." And we did. I was shooting pool with tears flowing onto the table. It was the most emotional thing. And my mother was crying terribly, too. Even though we weren't Catholic, my mother gave me a Saint Christopher medal before I left. I wore it all the time I was in the war. I felt I had protection. Honestly, I never felt as I left that I wasn't coming back. I assumed I was coming back. I left from the post office in Pittsburgh. My mother and dad were waving goodbye that night as I marched down to the train station....

My brother, Glenn, was already in Nashville when I arrived and we ended up being in the same class, 44 A. I had never been able to go up in an elevator for fear of heights, and here I was in the air force! Our initial training was on a Steerman PT-17, double-winged, open cockpit plane. My first flight was on July 5, 1943. We took off, and I was in the rear seat, with the instructor in the front seat. Each of us had a joystick that came up between our legs. The instructor was controlling the plane, and I was supposed to get the feel of it from the joystick on my side. But I wasn't even touching it because I was holding onto the sides of the plane for dear life! The instructor made my joystick ram hard into my left leg to get my attention. He said to me, "Get your goddamned hands off the side of the airplane and on the stick!"

In September, at Malden Army Air Field in Missouri, we went into a Bultee BT-13A, a single engine with a closed cockpit. Then on to Stuttgart, Arkansas, where we flew a twin engine, Beechcraft AT-10 VH. I got my wings there on January 4, 1944.

My first ride in a B-17 was January 21, 1944, at Chanute Field in Chicago. That's when my B-17 training began. The end of my B-17 transitional training was on March 10, 1944, just after my nineteenth birthday. My brother, Glenn, and I soloed together in Fort Worth, Texas.

I was the pilot of a B-17 crew in the Eighth Air Force, 381st Bombardment Group, 585th Squadron. In June we went to Gulfport, Mississippi, for the training of the pilots with their crews. Each crew had a meeting. If there was any objection from any crew member that he didn't want to fly with a particular pilot, they were kind enough to remove him. Prior to this meeting, I had a complaint about the way I was practicing my landings. The landing pattern required a certain kind of turn, and the colonel watching us said I was taking too wide a turn. He told me that when we got overseas there would be so many planes coming in that there wouldn't be that much time to spend on landing. The next day when they observed us, I made it quicker, but I turned so fast we were in almost a stalled position, but we were immediately on the runway. After that, my crew had its meeting. The flight engineer, Sergeant Brantley, came to me and said they had met and after seeing the way I handled the landing on instructions from headquarters, the crew knew they would be safe with me. This gave me the confidence I needed as a young pilot. I needed to know my crew felt they could rely on me to fly the damned plane. I probably did a better job in tough situations knowing my crew had faith in my abilities. Even though we had commissioned officers up in the nose on our crew, Brantley turned out to be the leader.

After being in Gulfport, I left with my crew from Langley Field in Virginia on August 19, 1944, to go overseas. But before we could leave, I spent a week recovering from a tonsillectomy performed by a pharmacist and a doctor's wife. While I was recovering, my brother was shipped out with another bomb group. This was the first time we had been separated since our training began.

With my crew, we first flew to Bangor, Maine; then to Goosebay, Labrador; then to Iceland and Wales; finally, we took a train to our air base in Ridgewell, England, arriving on September 7, 1944. My first combat mission was on September 17, which I flew as co-pilot. On September 21, I flew my first combat mission as pilot to Mainz, Germany. I flew a total of thirty-five missions.

We took off in the dark all the time, but we never flew a mission or landed in the dark. There were no lights over England then. Everything was blacked out. I did have to do a night solo for 1.3 hours. When I flew it, we got lost in the darkness, and finally spotted a river and followed it back to our air base. There were no landing lights, just a fire at the end of the runway.

In the mornings, we sat in our hut smoking cigarettes as they wiped the snow off the airplanes and loaded the bombs. I learned that to smoke a cigarette provided great tension relief, and everybody was doing it. Eighteen planes would get into formation, with the lead plane taking off first, usually a colonel or some highfalutin officer, and he would begin circling. They gave each group of eighteen planes a color. As the lead planes went up, they shot flares of different colors and we had to find the one with our color to know which one to join. There were hundreds of planes going up trying to find their leaders to get into formation. Before we even got over enemy territory, we had this rather risky feat. And there was a time element involved in doing this because the bombings were time coordinated. To add to the risk, the winter weather in England was almost always bad, either raining, snowing, misting, or foggy. When we first got up and were in formation, we had to go through an overcast together. They told us to be sure and hold altitude, direction, and speed as the eighteen planes were wingtip to wingtip in formation. We were to maintain position and not deviate up or down. I saw some accidents on these ascents. When we finally broke through the overcast, it was a real revelation.

On a mission to Merseburg, we had to leave the formation and fly back alone because an engine propeller was windmilling. I couldn't feather it because the oil was ruptured. I landed the plane, but everybody bailed out quickly because they thought it was going to explode. The flames had been coming over the cowling all the way across the Channel, and we had expected to explode at any minute. This was a nerve racking trip, as we had flown almost two hours in flames.

The most important thing I could do in a dangerous situation was to stay calm. You just have to keep going and see it through. During our missions, we were hit with a lot of flak, but we had very little aerial attacks. We were lucky.

On Christmas Eve 1944, we were able to celebrate because we didn't have to fly the next two days. Everybody got loaded.

Another time we had a colonel leading us, and he lead us right through a flak field. We had to leave the formation and fly it alone because the concussions of flak were felt right under the fuselage.

Once my navigator turned to say something to me, and just as he did, a piece of flak went right across his turned face and took off part of his eyebrow. If he hadn't turned his head, it would have gone right through him.

There were men on the flight crews who couldn't take it and ended up in mental hospitals. On our crew, we didn't worry about getting shot. We always had a lot of fun. I don't remember any of our guys ending up mentally unsound.

On our nineteenth mission to Cologne, Germany, we taxied out to the runway and prepared for take-off. After going over the check list, everything seemed to be in order to proceed down the runway. Standing between the co-pilot and me, Sergeant Brantley, the flight engineer, called off ground speeds so I could determine when to pull back on the stick for take-off. The B-17 stick had a pin through it to keep the elevators in the tail section from flapping in the wind while the plane was parked on the ground. Somehow, I had forgotten to remove the pin which made lift-off impossible. As we neared the end of the runway and Sergeant Brantley gave the O.K. for lift-off, I tried to pull back on the stick, but it would not budge. Sergeant

Brantley immediately recognized that the pin had not been removed, dove down and removed the pin just as we reached the end of the runway, allowing a take-off without further incident. It is quite evident that Sergeant Brantley saved the lives of ten men and one B-17. There were many acts of heroism during the war that were never documented; however, this one affected me personally, and I will never forget Sergeant Brantley and his response to this emergency situation.

On one of the raids to Brux, Czechoslovakia, we lost one of the gas tanks to flak and had to land in Brussels, Belgium. Fortunately, Belgium had been liberated by that time and was in friendly hands. Otherwise, we would have had to land in German territory.

One brave act that took place on our plane was when the mechanics of the bomb release malfunctioned, and the flight engineer, Brantley, had to go back into the bomb bay area with the doors open below him, and manually release the armed bombs one at a time. There wasn't more than a plank to stand on while he performed this job. That took guts. And this happened numerous times, on several occasions. We had to get rid of those bombs because we couldn't fly back to England and land with them. I would have never had the nerve to go back there, stand over the wide open space, and kick out armed bombs. I didn't have to tell him to do it. He knew if the bombs hung up it was his job, not mine.

In flying, my biggest fear was the possibility of having to evacuate the ship. We boarded the plane through a small opening into the nose where we boosted ourselves up. We were told in order to bail out that we should lower our head and shoulders back through that hatch and just fall out. I didn't think I could do that unless there were flames biting at my rear. I couldn't imagine poking my head and shoulders out that hole into the wide open space and just letting go, then hoping that the parachute worked!

* * *

As I reflect, my father was a hero, although when he was living, I didn't think he was. Now that he's been gone for twenty years, I realize how much he knew for having had only an eighth grade education. In many respects, he was a lot smarter than I am. He had a lot of common sense.

Thirty years ago, he wanted us to invest our excess money in the stock market. Having made myself the leader in our family business, I told him if we were going to invest any further money it would be in our own business, not the stock market. At that time, the market was around 800; today it's at 9000. Back then, I didn't think it would ever reach 1000. Our wealth would have been greatly enhanced if I had followed his idea. He knew the possibilities of the stock market, and I was too dumb too realize it. I have great respect for him about that. I would have been a lot better off today if I would have listened to my father back then. Honestly. My father had great foresight.

* * *

Sometimes I regret that when I came back from the war I didn't join the commercial airlines. All I would have had to do is take a physical exam and get a commercial license. When I was home for a couple of years, I heard about the salaries they were making and wondered if I shouldn't have stayed in it. After I came home from the war, I never got on another airplane until 1966. And then I was forced to because I had to travel for my job. Before that, I traveled only by car or train just to avoid flying.

I went to college on the G.I. Bill and got a degree in business administration. My outlook was to become something at which I could be successful. After college, I went into my father's plumbing and heating business, then into the automobile business for a time, and then back into the family business where I finished out my career. From the time I was thirty-one years old, I raised four kids and put them through college. I was able to afford to own a decent home and provide a decent living for my family. What better to be remembered for in life?

* * *

Being in the service for two and a half years under the guidance, strict supervision, and regimentation of superiors made me grow up fast and be a better person. I would recommend it for any young person straight out of high school. It provides guidance and maturity.

Something that's funny to me is how in sports today they talk about twenty-two year old players being too young to play a position. I was still nineteen when I flew my last mission. It was kind of frightening at the time! I remember writing to my mother telling her I had a twenty-seven year old

Leonard E. Rojohn

man back in the fuselage at the gunnery. At the time, I thought he was terribly old for me to have under my wing.

* * *

I am proud my brother and I were involved in a situation that helped to preserve democracy and win the war against Hitler. There were a lot of young fellows who risked their lives. That was patriotism. But when I went, I was just doing what the government expected me to do- my job.

CHAPTER NINETEEN

BILLIE JOSHUA SEAMANS

NOVEMBER 18, 1998

I grew up hard, sometimes near starvation. It wasn't easy. There were seven children in our family and it was during The Depression. Our daddy, Pinkney Samuel Seamans, was a lawyer, and nobody paid a lawyer anything. He was the city attorney for twenty-five years. There were four sons in our family. My daddy was on the draft board, and he sent all four of us to the war. That way there was not a man in the town who could say, "You sent my son, what about yours?" My brother, Glen Seamans, was the first boy to leave and the first boy to be killed from McGehee, Arkansas. The street called Seamans Drive is named after him. We were born and raised on Orange Street, and that's the street which was renamed. In 1942, I was the second of my family to be drafted. I was twenty-one years old at the time.

From Little Rock, Arkansas, we were taken by train down to St. Petersburg, Florida, where we took our basic training. I found out I was going to be in the air force during the train ride. Some men came by and announced to us, "Boys, you're in the air force." There were about four hundred of us staying in a hotel in downtown St. Petersburg. One of my friends from home was in my group. His name was Thomas Lee Jarrett. Our serial numbers were only one digit apart, so I knew his as well as my own. One day they asked for volunteers for aerial gunnery school. Six out of four hundred stepped out, and I was one of them. They dismissed the rest, and the six of us went in to see the sergeant. We stood in line, with me first. The sergeant asked for my name, rank, and serial number, without ever looking up. I gave him the name Thomas Lee Jarrett and the appropriate information. He never looked up, just kept writing. So, I returned to the end of the line. As the last one in the line, I gave the sergeant my own information on the second time around. When I got back upstairs, Thomas Lee wanted to know what we had been doing. I informed him that he had just volunteered for aerial gunnery school! He was sent to Keesler Field in Mississippi and was put in dive bombers. He later told me that everytime he went into a dive, all he could think of was me.

I went to gunnery school in Fort Myers, Florida, then was shipped to Oklahoma City, Oklahoma. We were put in A-20 planes. The A-20 was a twin-engine fighter bomber which was real fast. Our training was skip bombing at low, low altitude, from fifty to one hundred feet off the ground or water. We'd go down the Red River toward Amarillo, Texas, and fly over the dried up river bed. When we came to a bend in the river where there were trees, we'd have to pull up to go over those trees.

Then we were on our way to Russia with a lot of winter equipment on our planes. But before we could leave, we found out that Rommel was cutting up so bad in the Sahara Desert in North Africa that our destination would be changed. All the winter equipment was removed from our planes. Instead of taking the northern route, we headed south. But I never reached my destination. We made it to Puerto Rico and stayed there about three days, then took off again for Natal, Brazil. We were flying in a squad of seven planes. About one hundred miles out to sea, our plane ran into problems. We turned back toward Puerto Rico, leaving the other planes. We were at about ten thousand feet altitude. We kept going down and down, losing altitude. We finally had to salvo everything. There were twin 30-caliber machine guns on a pin weighing about three hundred pounds. I got down and pushed that sucker overboard. Then the one hundred seventy-five pound life raft went over. Then our clothes and everything went. All I could think about was a picture in there of a girl I'd met from Oklahoma City! But out it went. We continued to lighten the load, but the plane kept dropping. The pilot told us we weren't going to make it back to Puerto Rico, that we were going to have to bail out. We planned to bail out when we got down to a thousand feet. And I couldn't swim either. But at a thousand feet, first Jimmy Burns bailed, as from my knees I watched his parachute open. Then at nine hundred feet, out I went. Of course, I had never bailed out of an airplane before. When I landed in the water, I became tangled up in my parachute. And that's how they found me. I stayed out there six hours in shark-infested waters. A U.S.Navy PT boat picked me up, and a fishing boat picked up Jimmy. They saw my parachute on the swell of a wave and that's how they were able to find me. I was hollering, "Help!" even before anybody was around to hear me. After I hit the water and went under, I inflated my Mae West flotation device which kept my head up and knees sticking out. I tried to get my knife out of my escape kit in order to cut myself loose from the parachute. But when I tried, I lost everything out of the kit. It was a good thing because it was the parachute that lead them to find me. When I hit, I lost my shoes. It looked like the strings were cut with a razor blade. The stem and the crystal were knocked off my watch, but the watch was still on my arm. When they tried to pull me up the first time, I was so weak I fell right back into the ocean. They got me up on the second try. They had to just drag me up on the deck. The pilot crashed in a water landing about two hundred yards off the coast of Puerto Rico and he survived. But if we had stayed on the plane, we would have been killed. We bailed about fifteen miles out to sea. We were way out there. They got us back to Puerto Rico and then sent us back to Miami, Florida. Meanwhile, back at home, my mother had awakened during the middle of the night on that same day and knew something was wrong. She got out of bed and got down on her knees to pray. Although it was daylight where we were, it was the middle of the night at home. She told me about it when I got back from the war. Prayer does work.

Thirty days later, we picked up another plane and were off again. But we crashed on the tip end of Cuba at Antigua Bay. There was a tiny little landing strip. We went through thickets and everything and ended up in a crash with the nose end of the plane sticking up in the air. All the nose gear was torn out. I jumped out of the hole thinking the plane might explode. Usually it was three feet to the ground, but the position of the plane made that jump more like twenty feet. I hit on my stomach just like a cat. I didn't feel anything. Then I started running until I was about a hundred yards from the plane. The three of us watched the plane, but nothing happened. So, we went back and got all our stuff out. We were there for ten days before we were picked up. Finally, a small plane arrived and brought a bulldozer and pulled our plane back up on the runway of that little strip. They brought new nose gear and the instructions, and the three of us installed it. The pilot was able to take off, even with the fuselage all warped. We followed in the small plane to Camaguey, Cuba, where we spent thirty days. It was a millionaire's vacation. We stayed in a hotel downtown and the three of us had a big time. The Cubans thought the Americans were really something then, so we had everything we ever wanted. We worked on the plane a little bit more, but we didn't realize the side of the plane was wrinkled. We flew that thing from Camaguey, Cuba, back to Homestead, Florida.

We thought they'd be glad to see us, but they were mad! They didn't care if we died or not- we'd torn up two planes, and hadn't reached our destination yet! They put us in the hospital and gave us physical examinations. I was homesick, and while I was in the hospital I got mad and started saying I was going to go home after I got out of that hospital. I said I didn't care if I was AWOL or what. There was a guy in the bed next to me who was discharged the day before me. When we got our discharges from the hospital, we were told to report to headquarters. When we got there, we went into the commander's office. The commander was the guy who had been in the bed next to me! And he was a full colonel. He said to me, "Seamans, you're not going to go AWOL, are you?" I said, "No, sir!" He said he would let us go home for two weeks vacation because it would take that long to review the papers in order to tell if we three were fit to fly.

After two weeks, we were ready to go overseas. They wouldn't give us another plane because we'd already torn up two. They shipped us over in a C-54 Transport. We finally arrived at our destination in Africa five months after our initial departure. When we got there, they assigned us to B-17s: Fifteenth Air Force, 301st Bombardment Group, 419th Bomb Squadron. Our job for the first week was to clean the outdoor latrines. Then they assigned me to a plane. I was the lower ball turret gunner on twelve missions.

There were three photographers in a bomb group on each mission. This was to make sure at least one photographer got back with pictures. One day, all the photographers were lost. So, I volunteered to be a photographer, since it was always something that interested me. They gave me thirty days of training on how to operate the camera and all that kind of stuff. Then I started flying as a photographer, making pictures of combat scenes and bomb targets. My new position was as photographer-gunner. My camera was called a K-17 and it shot a nine-by-nine negative. There was a handheld camera, a K-20, which shot a four-by-five negative. I'd carry it back with me to the waist gun position and shoot aerial scenes. I remember one time, it got rough, and I laid that K-20 camera down and got my hands on the gun, thinking, "To hell with pictures!"

I never had just one crew. I was assigned to a different ship each day. A group of planes was about five or six squadrons; each squadron was six planes in two elements; and an element was three planes, one lead ship and two wing ships. I was always put in the lead ship, second element. During that time of the war, a crew was made up of nine men, and the photographer would make number ten. After I was through making pictures on a mission, I would man the waist gun or radio gun and let the radio operator return to his duties. Most of the time I manned the radio gun, the one coming out the top. My place in the plane was in the radio room. I could open my camera well, which was like a little bomb bay door, and stick my camera through to see the target and everything. The camera was electrically operated. I would shoot the first shot once I saw the bombs about five hundred feet below me. Then I would shoot every five seconds after I saw the first bomb flash. That would give me a series of pictures. After we came in from the mission, I had to process the film and print the pictures myself, and have them into headquarters by ten o'clock that night. There were two ground men who worked as photography assistants. We made about eight copies of each photo. They wanted to see what was going on, the percentage knockout. If we didn't hit it, we'd have to go back and hit that target again. If it was a good knockout, then we could go to another area.

A dental surgeon, Captain Gordon S. Sanctuary from New York, made a mask for me to wear while I was shooting pictures. I had trouble with my eyes freezing. When you look down and the wind is blowing at 170 miles per hour in your face, at thirty degrees below zero, yours eyes water and the tears freeze. In fact, when I would rub my eyes, all my eye lashes would break off because they were frozen together. I tried to wear goggles, but they fogged up on me and I had to take them off. Captain Sanctuary used a full-face rubber covering from a gas mask and put two goggles together with a vacuum between them. He said he got the idea for the double lenses remembering how he used to fix storm windows at home in the winter. This way I could have my face and eyes covered, and it wouldn't freeze or fog up. And I could see!

Some of our targets were Steyr, Austria, and Regensburg, Germany, and Athens, Greece, and Budapest, Hungary. We were based out of North Africa at first, then moved to Foggia, Italy. We hit all the Balkans from there:

Hungary, Greece, and Bulgaria, then Austria, Germany, France. We never hit Berlin, the Eighth Air Force took care of that. I flew a total of fifty missions.

On January 11, 1944, we were on our way to Athens, Greece. The German Navy was in Pireaus Harbor and we wanted to get them. When we took off, there were two groups of B-17s with about forty-five planes in each group. We crossed the Adriatic Sea toward Greece and ran into an overcast of dense clouds that was about seven thousand feet thick. We went into it in close formation, which was bad. We should have spread out. Two planes got in trouble and turned to go back. They should have turned right, but made a fatal left turn, coming across our group of planes. Seven of our planes crashed into each other because they couldn't see. We flew at a forty degree climb, straight, no turning. While we were doing that, we'd hit little pockets and I could see pieces of airplanes in the open cloud pockets. I was looking out the top of the plane from the radio room. While I was looking, another B-17 went right across us at about twenty feet. I almost died! I thought for sure he was going to hit us, but he missed. When we came out of the overcast, there were only three planes in our group left. Some had crashed, some had turned back, and some had made it. I was in the lead ship, not far from our target. But we ran into fighters and they jumped us. The guns on our plane were frozen from being in the overcast at twenty-one thousand feet. Two other B-17s with heaters on their guns were able to take shots at the fighters. We saw about twelve planes from another group that had made it and we got in with them. In close formation, we were able to fight off the fighter planes. We made the target and bombed the harbor. On the turn back, we separated from the other group of planes. Then our three planes got separated, and we were alone. We were over the Adriatic Sea trying to make it back to Italy. We were flying real close to the water, about five hundred feet, when we hit a rain storm. The navigator wasn't sure where we were. We came upon an American hospital ship along with others. They were in battle formation and didn't know who we were. We began firing out the colors of the day to identify ourselves so they wouldn't shoot at us. The colors of the day were different each day, either red, blue, green, or white flares. Whatever color was established would identify you as friendly and not to be fired upon. So, we were able to go on. We finally came to Italy and we were about two hundred miles south of our base at Foggia. We began to follow the coast and I remember seeing Mount Etna. I could see where the old lava flow had come down the volcano. We landed just about dark, I got to my tent, and found the guys had already ransacked my private belongings. We had been given up for lost. They were shocked to see me walk in. They had to give all my stuff back to me. Even after all that, I still had work to do getting the film processed. It had to be in that night. Our bomb group got a Presidential Citation for that raid.

We went to Regensburg, Germany, to bomb the aircraft factories. Fighters jumped us and shot fourteen planes out of our group. "Tail-end Charlie" was the name given to the planes on the outside ends of the group, and these planes had the most chance of being shot down. There were two squadrons, twelve planes, behind me, and all of them got shot down, along with two wing ships. That left our plane as "Tail-end Charlie." Not a good position to be in. We made it back safely, but there was a great loss of fourteen planes carrying a crew of nine boys on each.

On February 25, 1944, we bombed the aircraft factory at Steyr, Austria. I got credit for shooting down one ME-109. I let him have a hundred rounds, the whole can of ammunition, with a 50-caliber machine gun. It was represented by a swastika on my bomber's jacket, along with one bomb for each mission.

Finally, in April of 1944, we headed back to the United States. When we flew from Foggia, Italy, across the Sahara Desert in North Africa, we had to fly at thirteen thousand feet because of the dust storms. The red dust rose up to almost twelve thousand feet. We flew right on top of that dust. The oxygen was very thin. We landed in Dakar, Africa, then flew eighteen hundred miles over water to Natal, Brazil. When we got to Natal, we were down to two engines. Two had conked out on us. We started dropping from ten thousand feet. As we approached Natal, we were right at five hundred feet. We weren't too worried about it. We were sitting around playing poker, laughing and talking, not worried about anything. We knew we could make it on just one engine if we had to, but two were better! We circled once and landed. Then we had to work on those two engines before we could get back in the air and on to Puerto Rico. After we got to Puerto Rico, everybody bought a case of rum, which was four gallons. We weren't supposed to bring that much of it into the United States. We also stashed some personal belongings in ammunition cans. This was meant to keep certain things hidden from the plane inspectors after we got back. We put all that rum behind each engine where there was a space to hide it. We had a total of eight cases. We were allowed one gallon of rum apiece and claimed that to the inspectors in Homestead, Florida, but as soon as the inspectors went away, we started unloading! We used all that rum to have a big party in Miami. We had a good time and made a lot of friends with that rum.

* * *

When I was about fourteen years old, I was frog gigging up at Tillar Brake. I was wading in the water about twenty feet out from the shore, looking back at the bank, and saw some rippling water. I walked to it and shined my light down on it. It was an eel and a water moccasin trying to swallow each other. I watched and watched, and wished I could get a picture of that. Of course, I didn't know anything about how to get a picture at that time. That created something in my mind that I might want to learn something about photography.

I was twenty-three years old when the war was over and I got out. I met and married Dorothy Barrett, my sister's friend, within two weeks of my return home.

The war gave me the opportunity to get into photography. When I got back from the war, I went to photography school. Then I worked for Mrs. Drummond in McGehee at her photography studio. After that, I worked for twenty years with International Harvester Company. I photographed farm equipment. One year, the agriculture business was hit real hard and almost had a depression. The company began making cuts and I lost eighty percent of my work. So, I quit. Then I farmed for one year, and went broke. That was 1970. I lost everything but my home. That's when I decided to put in my own photography studio... at age fifty, flat broke. It was my second chance in life, and what I have loved the most.

I have always been patriotic. I was patriotic from the beginning of the war. I was ready to go, ready to fight. I still have a lot of patriotism. In the American Legion, we are responsible for putting out flags on our streets, and we also put out three hundred flags in cemeteries on veterans' graves. We recently dedicated a large flag at the cemetery which is lighted and flies twenty-four hours a day. This is how we can shape the future of patriotism.

It's important to spend time with your children. I always spent time with my three boys. We hunted, fished, and attended ball games. If you participate in your children's activities, you won't have as many problems with them.

Billie Joshua Seamans

Nowadays, I'm doing the same thing for my grandchildren. It shows that I put them first, and it's good for them to see that.

One secret to a good life is to stay active. It'll keep you young. I won't retire until I have to. I want to be remembered as an honest, energetic fellow, someone who doesn't give up.

My advice to the younger generation is to honor your parents, get a good education, and go to church. If you do all those things, you'll live a good life. It all depends on *you*.

CHAPTER TWENTY

ROBERT MAIER SMITH

JULY 28, 1998

In the spring of 1942, I was at Ouachita Baptist College in Arkansas. Pearl Harbor had already happened. I didn't think the United States would really get into the war. I wasn't worried about it. But the drafting started later that year. And I didn't want to be drafted. I found out I could sign up in the reserve corps. This meant I would be in the service, but I wouldn't be called for a year. So, I signed up, and that kept me in college another year. That probably saved my life.

I went to Camp Maxey, Texas, for basic training. I was in the ASTP (Army Specialized Training Program) which would send me to college to be an engineer. I went to the University of Arkansas; then I got an appointment to West Point. I was thinking, "Boy, I've got this thing made!" I was sent to Lafayette College in Easton, Pennsylvania, an old, old school, which was to prepare me for West Point. I had to take a test, and I missed it by one point. This kept me out of West Point. They sent me directly to Camp Livingston near Shreveport, Louisiana, for more training. Then I was put on the Queen Elizabeth, which had been converted to a troop ship, and sent to Glasgow, Scotland. I was on the front end of the ship in a rough sea. It seemed like I'd go up in the air for thirty minutes before coming back down. I got sick as a dog. When we got to Glasgow, we were in pup tents for about a week before they sent us by train to the southeast coast of England, then we boarded ships and sailed across the North Sea to Omaha Beach.

We came in many days later than the troops who landed at Normandy Beach on D-Day. The beach had been cleaned up. There weren't any wrecks and not much barbed wire. The cliffs were so high and so steep, I wondered how those fellows got up that hill. I was glad I didn't have to go up that hill under fire. When the men before me went up, they were shot by the Germans at the top who were in fortified pill boxes. Our troops were shot point blank. I was glad it wasn't me. I was sent over there for cannon fodder, a replacement for infantry casualties. It wasn't a cheerful outlook. I was twenty years old at that time.

We climbed the beach and marched about twenty-five miles through the area where the Germans had used the hedgerows for fighting. Of course, by now, the Germans were gone. Then we were put on trucks. When we went through Paris, it was night. We couldn't see anything. We came to a point where we were sent either toward Metz, a German fortress occupied by the German Army, or toward Switzerland. At this time, all our troops were sent over as replacements and were assigned to the Third Army or the Seventh Army. We were assigned to the Seventh Army, the Forty-fourth Infantry Division, 114th Regiment, and we went to Nancy, France, in Alsace-Lorraine. The people who lived there had two flags. When the Germans came through, they put out the German flag. When the Americans came through, they put out the French flag.

Our campaign was in and through the Voges Mountains which were strictly wooded. I remember one time our company was traveling on one side of a wooded valley, about halfway up the mountainside, and going in a big long line. The front of the company ran into some Germans and were under fire. Consequently, we all stopped. And when we stopped like that, each of us had a little shovel in our backpack, and we'd get it out and start digging. We dug a foxhole every time we stopped. It was just routine; self-protection. Anyway, I was just a-digging, and out of the corner of my eye, I saw a captain and a lieutenant. The lieutenant was a forward artillery observer. They said for us fellows to come with them. I kept digging. I didn't want to go with them. One of them came over and tapped me on the shoulder, and said, "Hey, soldier, did you hear me?" He took eight of us almost to the top of the mountain to a large brush pile. The captain and lieutenant followed me to the right; the rest of the men went to the left. About a hundred yards past the brush pile, we heard the sounds of three mortars. They started hitting all around us. It hit the tree that I was under and knocked some limbs down, just enough to scare the heck out of me. The next one hit so close it splashed mud on me. It made a hole in the ground about a yard in diameter. If you got hit by one of those, you were gone. I had my head down, praying, of course. I thought the next one would be down on top of me. The thumping of the mortars in the distance stopped, so I knew there probably wouldn't be anymore to hit. When I looked up, that captain and lieutenant were running back down the hill. They didn't say anything to me. They hadn't gone fifty yards before I passed them up! I beat them back down to where I'd been digging my foxhole, and I started digging again. They waited there for a while for the other boys to come back. No one showed up. So, the captain sent some people up there to find out what happened. Several had been killed, and some were wounded. One of the boys who stumbled back down was "crazy," I guess what you'd call shell shocked.

The background noise during all this time was one continuous roar, like a thunderstorm. It was the sound of artillery from both sides. I heard this for the entire six months I was in combat. After that incident, every time that boy who came back from the mountain would hear a shell going overhead, he'd hit the ground and start crying. It was just pitiful. He'd been a brave boy up until he saw those around him get killed, and he'd come so close. After that, just the sound of a shell would send him into orbit. They had to send him back because he was no longer fit for combat.

I saw several Germans who'd been hit by shells. Some were decapitated. Their helmets were completely torn up by the shells. But most of the time, the injured had been removed.

One time we'd captured half a town. It was divided by a railroad. We were on one side, and the Germans were on the other. We'd gotten into and occupied the houses. Most of the time, we wanted to be in the basement because the top floors were vulnerable to artillery fire. I was on watch and standing at the window when I saw a German. I could tell it was a German by his long overcoat which came down almost to his feet. I saw him get up out of a hole and I took a shot at him. He started running, so fast that his overcoat went straight out behind him. He fell and I never saw him anymore.

With us was a Jewish boy. Everybody loved him. He was kind of peculiar, but harmless. You'd never think of him wanting to fight, but he could. It was nighttime at the same place. This boy had to go outside to relieve himself. He went down the steps into the front yard. It just so happened that a German platoon was on patrol and was coming in to feel us out, see where we were. They shot the boy and he ran for the house. He fell down the steps into the basement where we were. He was dead when he hit the bottom.

Subsequently, we went across the railroad and ran off the Germans with artillery and rifle fire. We captured two young German infantrymen. My sergeant was bad; and he was mad at the Germans for killing the Jewish boy. He took the Germans out behind a barn and shot them in cold blood.

I could never condone anything like that. All he had to do was hold them and send them back to the rear lines. But he just killed them in cold blood.

We went on through that area, and approached a town. We could see a big orchard, many acres all around the town. We were all spread out and approaching in one big line. We saw a haystack way across the field, close to the town. The haystack exploded. We could see Germans flopping that hay back. They opened fire on us with what appeared to be a 20mm antiaircraft gun. Instead of aiming at each man, they aimed at each tree. When each shell exploded, it would get several men at one time. We all hit the ground and called for artillery. But the Germans high-tailed it. They left their guns and everything. My sergeant crawled back to me and said, "Hey, Smitty, they got me in the leg." I saw where it was bleeding. It didn't look death defying. But he told me he was going back for first aid, and he said I was now the sergeant.

We went on into the town. All the people of the town were in the basement because they knew the town was being fought for. We found a good house. We hadn't had a house for a long time to sleep in. We spent the night. Each of us took turns standing guard for two hours. Two hours on, two hours off.

Then we went on. It was night and we were in the Voges Mountains. The captain was behind us. Someone said, "We're lost. And the captain knows we're lost." We thought we were probably behind German lines and that we would have to wait until morning to know our location. I was dead tired. It had been raining a lot and the ground was mud. I wondered how I was going to sleep on the mud. I whacked a bunch of evergreen limbs with my bayonet. I laid them down and made a nice pile, and put my overcoat on top of that. I lay down and put my raincoat over me. I was able to stay off the cold, wet earth that way. The few hours I got to sleep were the best! I had learned how to improvise. Being on the front line, I had even gotten used to the constant roar of the shells.

We found out where we were and we made contact with the Germans. They must have heard us coming because they started shelling us with mortars. My buddy and I started digging our foxhole. He said to me, "You little son-of-a-bitch, you get out of the way. You can't dig." He was a great big old fellow from Pennsylvania. So, I said, "Okay, you dig, and I'll go get some limbs to put over the top of the foxhole." As soon as I got back to the hole, the shells started getting close. We hit the bottom of the hole and covered up. One of the shells hit so close to us, we thought the next one was going to come right in the hole. We started praying. I was praying Methodist; he was praying Catholic. We finally opened our eyes when we heard the explosions lessen up. We looked over at the opening where we'd come down into the hole. There was a white vapor floating down. I thought, "Oh, my God, it's poisonous gas!" And we'd thrown away our gas masks. I looked down at the palms of my hands and they were luminescent. I said, "Oh, it's eating my hands up!" But it didn't hurt. Then I thought back to my Boy Scouts days, and I knew what it was- fox fire. It was from my being out there digging around old rotten logs and rooting around for limbs. It had gotten on my hands and that's what the glow was. I knew then we had nothing to worry about. I'd thought it was poisonous gas eating us up. The vapors coming down in the hole was the smoke from the shells. That's how close they'd hit to us. We spent the rest of the night in pretty good shape, although the shelling continued throughout the night. We were always afraid one of the shells would land in the foxhole with us.

I was one of the fortunate ones who had acquired a pair of galoshes. Our G.I. boots weren't waterproof so there was no way to stay dry and warm in them, but the galoshes worked great for me. I was so proud of those galoshes! That night, in the foxhole, I took off my galoshes and set them right outside the foxhole. I awoke at daylight and when I went to get my galoshes they were frozen solid. There wasn't anyway to get them on. I looked around. There was a shell hole about five feet in diameter about eight feet from our foxhole. It must have rained into that shell hole, because it was full of water which had frozen over during the night. I tried to break through the ice with my galoshes in order to get them wet so I could thaw them out, but the ice would not break. My next idea solved two problems at once. I had a full bladder and was able to urinate on both galoshes enough to be able to thaw them. It worked out wonderfully!

At our next encounter, I was appointed along with a Mexican-American soldier to go way out in front about three hundred yards. We went to a designated foxhole that was already dug. On our left was a mine field, so we weren't worried about the Germans coming at us from that direction. About a hundred yards away was a machine gun that we were guarding. We took turns on watch. On my turn, suddenly a flare went off. It lit up everything bright as day. I could see what looked like a million Germans. They had on white snow suits. We hit the bottom of that foxhole. When I looked again, after the flare was gone, I could still see them. They were that close. We each had a BAR (Browning Automatic Rifle)and an M-1 thirty-caliber rifle on us and had to decide what to do. I knew that the machine gun outpost we'd been guarding had been abandoned because I saw the machine gunners previously retreat to the rear. The decision was that the two of us would not take on all those Germans. We left the foxhole and went back the three hundred yards to our command post. It was a big house with a stone fence around it. As we got close, I began saying, "It's Smitty, it's Smitty. Don't shoot, don't shoot!" We got behind the fence and saw that the Germans were still coming. We began shooting at them over the fence. One of their shells hit between us and the house. The Mexican-American soldier with me started yelling, "They hit me!" When I looked, I could see blood on his back side. They'd got him in the butt. I told him he wasn't hurt that bad and to keep on shooting.

Then we went into the house and went upstairs. I found a machine gun. I told one of the men I was Sergeant Smith and to load up that gun for me. I made him my ammunition man. The Germans had begun to attack again. I looked out the window and began firing. When I couldn't see what to fire at, I fired at their gun flashes. Then they started using tracer bullets. Those are the kind you can see the streaks. I'd duck behind the stone wall by the window and wait for about four of those streaks to whiz by my head, then I'd know it was safe to try to take some more shots at them. In the next room was a fellow we called the "antitank boy." He had a 37mm antitank gun, but he'd left it behind when he came back to the house. Now he was shooting with his rifle. We took turns firing. Just back and forth. It calmed down a little bit, and I realized I didn't hear him firing anymore. I went over to see about him and he'd caught a bullet right in the chest. He was dead as a doornail. I didn't know the man personally. He had on a watch, and I needed a watch worse than anything in the world. So, I borrowed his watch. If I'd known who he was, I would have written to his folks and told them about it.

I didn't rightfully steal his watch, I just borrowed it. I needed it a hell of a lot worse than he did.

Later that night, I was watching, and lo and behold, I looked out there and saw a shape. It would move a little bit here, a little bit there. I hollered, "What the hell you doing down there?" No answer. I shot. The next morning I saw a tree where someone had been behind shooting at me. That tree had bullet holes where I'd fired, from the bottom all the way up about six feet. I didn't find a German there, but there was a lot of blood. And there was a pair of binoculars and a canteen cup. I took those. I could tell the canteen cup had held schnapps. I guess they'd had to be fortified to jump off in the attack. We found about fifteen German casualties.

Subsequently, we were mounting an attack on a big scope of woods, and we had to jump off before daylight. We started moving through the woods, and spread out. We came to a railroad track in a gully which we had to cross. Just as someone in front of me started to cross, the Germans opened up on us with machine guns. It was dark, we couldn't see anything, and we were scared as hell. We didn't know what to do, so we didn't do anything. We just stayed in that gully where the railroad track was until they quit shooting. Some of our officers called in for artillery fire. The forward observer who was with us on the front line could phone back to the artillery which wasn't too far behind us, and tell them where to fire. So, he directed a lot of artillery fire in there, and the Germans who were manning the machine guns apparently left. I was never so proud of our artillery as that day. They really mopped those woods out, we thought. We advanced a long ways into the woods, and we were coming out on a kind of a plane it seemed. The artillery was still being fired over our heads. Then the German artillery began to return fire. Our command was to stop and dig in. I leaned my M-1 rifle up against a bush to start digging a foxhole. When I did, I felt something like an electric shock and heard a whirring sound right over my head. I hit the ground. I looked down and my hand was bloody. It was completely numb. A machine gun bullet went right through my hand and smashed my knuckle pretty bad.

When I saw what had happened to my hand, I called out to a man, just a kid, about ten yards from me. He was a new replacement who had never seen any action. He was a bug-eyed boy who wore real thick horn-rimmed glasses. He looked like a hoot owl crawling through the brush, coming toward me after I'd called him. I told him I'd been hit by a bullet in my hand

and needed him to wrap it up for me. He said, whimpering, "Those dirty S.O.B.'s shot you..." I told him to quit his crying and start wrapping. After he took care of me, I told him to stay put and I gave him the binoculars I had taken off the German on New Year's Night. I told him I'd be back to get them. I crawled and walked back several hundred yards to the command post where the captain was stationed. He directed me down the road where I would find help. I found a man in a Jeep who took me to the First Aid Station. When my hand was unwrapped, they saw gold chips from my class ring which were imbedded in the wound. It had taken my heavy McGehee High School class ring. I never saw it again. My hand was still numb at this time. It didn't start hurting until later. Then they put me in an ambulance with several other wounded G.I.s, including two wounded Germans. I didn't feel too good about those Germans being on there, but they were obviously critically injured, so I didn't worry about them. We were taken to a hospital where an operation was done on my hand.

From that hospital I was sent to a recovery area in Aix-en-Provence in southern France along the Mediterranean. While there, I contracted jaundice. After sweating that out, I got pneumonia which had to be treated with sulfa drugs. I wanted to go back with my outfit after I recovered, but in only a short time, the war was over. When everyone found out the war in Europe was over, they started shooting guns in celebration. It was dangerous and I didn't want to get hit so I crawled under the bunk.

Later, I was assigned to a ship and into a medical outfit. They were sending me to the South Pacific. We were a day out when we got news the war in Japan was over. Our course was changed immediately to New York City. From New York City, I was sent to Fort Chaffee, Arkansas, where I met up again with my old outfit, the Forty-fourth Division. I set out to find the young soldier I had given my binoculars to, only to find out he had sold them.

* * *

One thing I've thought about a lot since World War II is that it is terrible for any race or country to have wars that kill people. This has gone on for eons and eons. War is a terrible, terrible thing. Fellow human beings are killed, and it's the only way: to kill or be killed. There ought to be a better

Robert Maier Smith

way to solve problems. If God could only give us some direction that would eliminate war....

Patriotism is something you have to have. You do what you have to do to protect your country from destruction from outside evil forces. It's an obligation to do whatever is necessary. Although we did not want to go to war, we did not shirk the responsibility.

When we got close to death, we realized that we needed to make our lives count for something. We became mature. We returned from the war ready to build good lives for ourselves and others.

Before I went into the service, I lacked only a few hours having chemistry and mathematics degrees. After I returned, I changed my mind. I wanted a career where I would be dealing with people, so I went to law school and became a lawyer. It was a way for me too fulfill my yearnings and perhaps do something for humanity, too. Some people may disagree that this is the ultimate goal of the legal profession, but really it is. It's all about human rights.

I want to be remembered as a person who was called to duty and who fulfilled what I thought was my duty, doing the best under the circumstances. I've done my best to do my civic duties having served as city attorney for more then twenty years; served on the school board for twelve years; served on the city council for four years. I've guided my family as best I could and got them educated. These things reflect who I am. People who know me know my accomplishments. And my faults. One saying that has guided my life is "Do unto others as you would have them do unto you." If you can help others by doing things that are necessary in your community, then you'll have accomplished a whole lot and will have attained happiness in doing so.

CHAPTER TWENTY-ONE

LAL DUNCAN THRELKELD

DECEMBER 3, 1998

We were a generation who had come through a depression. Everybody was hungry, and military pay looked very appealing to a lot of guys. Especially after the attack on Pearl Harbor, the draft boards and recruiting stations were jammed full of men ready to go. They knew we had to get it over with.

I was born in Oklahoma City, Oklahoma, a long time ago. I've never been one to discuss my war experiences too much with anybody. I've never even been back to any of my cavalry reunions. There were four medical officers, and I'm the only one surviving.

I took advanced field artillery at the University of Oklahoma. I was a reserve officer when I graduated from medical school in 1940. I transferred to the medical corps where I was made first lieutenant, and was ordered to active duty July 1942. I was married in a military wedding ceremony at Fort Sam Houston Chapel on January 8, 1943.

I was Division Medical Supply Officer in the Ninety-fifth Infantry Division, then transferred to the Fifteenth Cavalry Regiment in January 1944. I didn't know anything about the cavalry. I knew about artillery, and I'd been trained in the infantry. But I was the only medical officer qualified for going overseas. Bingo! That's how I went over to the cavalry from the infantry. We left shortly thereafter.

The cavalry troops were elite. We had a high percentage of radio operators, code operators, and other highly trained personnel. Cavalry is for pooping and snooping. We were always out front. We were sent down before the actual Normandy Invasion to guard the troops that had been briefed. Once they were briefed on their mission, they were put under armed guard. Due to espionage, there were orders to shoot anybody who tried to leave the camp. We didn't want to tip off the Germans.

We were a cavalry regiment made of a cavalry group which consisted of two squadrons, the Fifteenth and the Seventeenth. Each squadron was commanded by a lieutenant colonel, and the group commander was a full colonel. Our group commander was John Reybold, and he was a character. He was a Special Service Officer at West Point. All the old regular army officers, like Patton, knew Reybold. In fact, those two had been to West Point together. They were two-year wonders. Reybold was a very impressive guy, a charming person. He was related to the Duponts and had a lot of influence politically and otherwise.

One time when we were out in the California desert in training, he made us all carry fly swatters and kill flies. On weekends, those of us who had transportation, would go into Palm Springs. He restricted all the officers to the camp area, and let the other men go in. He made the officers do all the clean-up like scrubbing latrines, just as though we were enlisted men.

Twelve days after D-Day found us at Utah Beach in France for the Normandy Invasion. We came in from behind and helped take Cherbourg. We lost Colonel Reybold on the first roadblock we hit after we went through Avranches, France. He was captured by the Germans and taken to the Channel Islands. All through the war, we thought he must be dead. After the war was over, Reybold showed back up in Germany. He'd been shot in the wrist, and I gave him a Purple Heart.

General Patton came in and took over the Third Army. We were Task Force A, the point of the Third Army. Patton told us our mission was to secure all the rail bridges over the estuaries in northern Brittany. Brest was an important port for supplies with excellent rail connections. Beautiful railroad bridges had been built over the estuaries. We were to capture those quickly so the Germans wouldn't blow them up. We bogged down in Saint-Malo and started a battle there. We ran into a lot of resistance. Another division was sent in to take over that battle, so we could continue on our own mission. We went through Avranches during the night where, during the

Saint-Malo breakout, a thousand-plane pattern bombing had devastated the place. As we went through all the small towns along our route, we captured over eight thousand prisoners. Patton had told us not to take any prisoners. He meant for us to kill them. The Free French took care of a lot of those prisoners by murdering them. As cavalry, we had no provision for taking prisoners. We had no place to put them. We couldn't put them on armored cars or tanks and keep fighting. We were breaking through, with no backup troops behind us. So, we couldn't leave them behind us either.

While at Morlaix, which was before Brest, we hit the Germans but we didn't mop them up. They re-formed, came in behind us, and caught us the next morning. We finally wiped them out. We made that mistake once, and they regrouped, attacking us from the rear the next morning. After that, we got a little tougher about killing them. We had two lieutenants court-martialed and sent back to the United States because they refused to kill. Still, we herded eight thousand prisoners back. We put them in a pen and put them under guard. Really, we didn't even have to pen them up. They were happy to be with us. Many were Polish youth who were drafted into the German Army.

Hitler ordered that Brest be defended at all costs. It was near Brest, on a Sunday, that some of own P-47s came in and dropped their bombs. We lost a whole platoon, all the men killed. One of the bombs went into a village church while mass was being conducted. I got one little old lady out of there whose legs had been blown off. It was terrible.

After Brest fell, they split our cavalry group. The Fifteenth Squadron stayed to contain the troops in Lorient and Saint Nazaire. My squadron, the Seventeenth, was sent on through Paris and up to Holland. We were then assigned to General Simpson's Ninth Army. The First Army, on our right flank, was having a hell of a time trying to clear the Germans out of the Hurtgen Forest, near Aachen and Maastrich. The fighting in the Hurtgen Forest was vicious. Right up on the Ruhr River was a dam and reservoir. The mosquito bombers had tried to blow it down, but had not succeeded. We were lined up along the Ruhr River unable to cross because we knew once we did, the Germans would bomb that dam and flood our rear. We were stalemate, fighting a war of attrition, waiting on the First Army to clear the Germans out of the Hurtgen Forest, which they did, but at a terrible cost. The First Army, First Division, said they were really three divisions: one division in the cemetery, one division in the hospital, and one division fighting. The

Third Division in Italy took more casualties than any other division in the army.

As the Germans collapsed, we got through Crozon. I was told about some wounded men, so I got on my Jeep and went up a little road. All at once, we came under 20mm fire. I climbed out of the Jeep and got down behind a low rock wall. They riddled my Jeep. It was destroyed. Then along came some tanks to wipe out the guns. The tanks took up the whole of that little narrow road. One was about to run over me. He was looking down the road at the target and didn't see me. I got my handkerchief out and began waving it until he saw me. He was able to steer around, and they went on down the road and knocked the gun out. I wasn't able to move from my position because the gun was still shooting at me.

We got shot up five different times by our own planes. I remember we shot down a German fighter that was trying to strafe us. I can just see the old boy now as he was came down in his parachute out in the middle of a mine field. He started waving at us. I wasn't about to go out and get him!

A wounded P-51 pilot was brought in to me. He was strafing when he flew by a church steeple. A sniper from that tower shot his engine and the pilot had to bail out. As he bailed out, the tail caught him and gashed his leg. They brought his parachute in with him. Nylon! Talk about something to trade with the French girls! A whole parachute! Doggone, if they didn't send a couple of air force guys two days later to get back that parachute. Anyway, I didn't get to cash in on the parachute.

We captured a German general. He was down in a concrete bunker and wouldn't come out. We wheeled a tank destroyer up to that bunker, pointed it down the stairway, and let it fire. Boy, that general came out of there then. He was in formal dress, wearing white gloves. Our tank commander told the general to give over his white gloves. The general acted haughty. So the tank commander stuck a forty-five pistol in his gut and got the gloves as a souvenir.

I took care of more German wounded than our own wounded. I remember one German boy they brought back was sitting on top of a Jeep hood smoking a cigarette. When I got him in there to check him, he'd been shot through the right lung. Somehow the wound had sealed itself. He didn't even have a pneumothorax. It went between his ribs and right out his back.

The most I usually had to do for the German wounded was give them a tetanus shot, maybe some morphine, then get them evacuated as fast as we could. We had twelve aidmen covering seven hundred-eighty fighting men. Four men and a Jeep driver stayed with me at the aid station. I put two men out in a halftrack ambulance with each troop. This was over a thirty-mile area. I had a 5-10 radio that didn't do me any good for communication. I finally threw it away. The halftrack ambulances would pick up the wounded, and then try to find us back at the aid station. The troopers could usually tell the ambulance drivers where we were located and how to get back to us.

One of my medical officers was a big fellow of Norwegian descent. When he got with us, he had two huge black eyes from a Jeep accident. I told him he looked like a zombie. He was a very interesting character, born in China to missionary parents, his father a doctor. I had to watch him because he didn't want to take care of a wounded German. His idea was, "To hell with him. Let him die." I don't think he ever did anything in a covert fashion, but he never lifted his hand to take care of a German.

Before the Normandy Invasion, I had gone to a special school near Birmingham, England, to learn about treating combat fatigue. It was run by the Menninger brothers, both psychiatrists. The Eighth Air Force had been in terrible combat for a year before we made the Normandy Invasion. These airmen were cracking up under combat fatigue, a euphemism for mental collapse. They were using shock therapy to treat these men; insulin shock and heavy sedation to try to get them back to fighting condition.

One man was a captain and the pilot of a B-17. His co-pilot resembled his kid brother. This co-pilot stopped a German bullet with his head and was killed instantly. The pilot cracked up over it.

Colonel Lindquist of our Seventeenth Squadron was the darling of officers, best pistol shot in the outfit, and in the regular army. They brought him back to me stiff as a poker, from hyperventilation, alkalosis, and tetany. I kept him sedated and carried him around in a halftrack for a couple of days. But he was absolutely ineffectual. We didn't get rid of him until we got clear up into Germany. He was just nothing. He had to be reclassified. Major McGraff from Texas took over as our commanding officer in Holland and Germany.

I went to London to get a supply of Purple Hearts before we went across. I had a whole box of Purple Hearts to give out, so I was real popular. Another reason I was real popular is that the Medical Supply Depot had an unlimited supply of rye whiskey. I requisitioned plenty of that to use for treating trench foot. I discovered after the Bulge, fighting in the winter, in the cold, that trench foot was a problem. But the men in my outfit never had that problem. I made them change their socks everyday. When the men were in the foxholes, I put small Coleman gasoline stoves in there, along with straw on the ground, to keep them warm and dry. This prevented anyone from getting trench foot.

Some wounds were self-inflicted. I had one guy who shot himself in the toe. Another fellow picked up a machine gun which had a round in it, butt first and muzzle first between his hands, and blew a hole right through his hand. Another guy was in an armored car with his machine gun pointed down, it went off and shot him through both hips. He died right there in my aid station.

I had begun my medical residency in gynecology before going to the war. I got to use some of that training while over there. One night in Brittany, we were in a convent courtyard for the night, and a Frenchman came charging up. Near as we could gather, his wife was having all kinds of problems. I went with him to his house, and the woman was in labor, so I delivered the baby. Later, I helped deliver two babies in Germany.

The only intravenous fluid I had in supply to give a man in shock was plasma. I had a pretty good supply. I learned on pulling men out of a burning tank or armored vehicle to give them that plasma in the femoral vein. There was no use wasting time looking for another vein. And there was plenty of morphine for pain. At Morlaix, during a blackout, some guys were brought in to me who had run into steel rails planted upright in the road by the Germans. They had been driving a six-by-six truck which held a gasoline powered refrigerator full of penicillin. I had heard of penicillin, but never saw it or used it. All I had was sulfadiazine to use for infection. I don't know what happened to that penicillin, but it was my first knowledge of its availability. They were using it back in the field hospitals.

Mostly, I administered first aid and got the wounded out of there. But once, I performed an appendectomy on a soldier in Holland. Then there were the hopeless cases like gunshots to the head. We couldn't do anything for them, and we lost a bunch.

We were in enemy contact for 125 straight days. It made us become insensitive, thinking, "Well, if I'm gonna get it, I'm gonna get it." We were just living from day to day. We began to get cynical about death because it was so prevalent.

The Germans had a shoe mine that was a little wooden box. It couldn't be located with a mine detector. It had a quarter of a pound of T.N.T. in it. It was like a mousetrap. It was propped up, and all you had to do was step on it and it would explode, shattering your legs. I took care of a bunch of guys with those injuries. Land mines killed so many. You wouldn't even have to be fighting to get killed. When the snow was on the ground, the Germans pushed wooden box mines up into the snow drifts. One boy was out looking for a box to send home souvenirs. He pulled one of those mines. It blew him to bits. I had to fish his liver out of a tree.

Being road-bound cavalry, we didn't go across fields as we traveled. On either side of the road were bar ditches. Germans would sow these ditches with antipersonnel mines. Then they set up a road block on a little rise. As we came along, they started firing at us, forcing our guys to peel off into the ditches full of mines. Our solution to that was the 75mm canister which we lined up with a bar ditch and fired it down, clearing out all the mines.

One of my aidmen was up with the cavalry troop on the road in Germany. They were hit at a road block. He rallied the soldiers and got them to fighting. He earned a Distinguished Service Cross for his effort. That was heroic. He was someone I handpicked to be with me as one of my twelve aids. They were all smart men and I never lost one of them, although two were wounded.

We had a priest and a lay minister. Father Walsh, our first priest, cracked up and I had to send him back. He was replaced by Father Neilly who was a tough Jesuit. He did all right. We nicknamed the priest and minister "Hook and Crook" because they were the best looters in the outfit. They had a Jeep with a one-ton trailer that carried their portable pump organ. The chaplain's assistant was also the Jeep driver and the organ player. We never lost a chaplain's assistant. He would have been hard to replace.

"Crook," the Protestant minister, joined our outfit at Brest. He reported to me at the aid station, which was out in the field. I told him to pitch his tent and get a bed roll. The son-of-a-gun had a rifle he'd gotten from somewhere. I said he wasn't supposed to have it, but he said he wasn't going to let someone slip up on him. He intended to keep it. During the night, "Crook" started howling and yowling during a nightmare. He was holding onto that rifle. We had to wrestle it away from him. That was the end of his rifle.

We were moving forward. I left the aid station, and hadn't gone two hundred yards, when a shell hit it. When the wounded were brought in, the priest and minister were always there to help. "Hook" was at the aid station when the shell came in. I told the Jeep driver to return. Smoke was coming out and the Germans were throwing everything they had at us. The shell that hit the station was a smoke shell. I initially thought the aid station was wiped out. When I got to Father Neilly, he had a shell fragment in his shoulder, so he got a Purple Heart.

"Hook," or Father Neilly, got to Paris near the war's end. Of course, he went to see Notre Dame Cathedral. He came back and told me how he was at the cathedral, remembering its history, in sublime thought, when a French prostitute approached him, completely exposing herself to him! He was in uniform and there was no way she could have known he was a priest. He was shocked.

In the little farming villages, the most educated man was always the priest who could usually speak English. One in Holland told me how upset he was that twenty girls in his village were pregnant, and the fathers were unknown.

If the Germans had been smart, they would have issued P-38s and Lugers to all the American soldiers. In the course of the war, I saw eighteen accidental fatal shootings by our men from playing with captured German pistols. In Holland, I went to the colonel and told him he had to get these non-issued guns out of the hands of these guys because they were killing themselves. He ordered all non-issued military equipment to be turned in. At that point in time, I had already collected for myself a sackful of pistols. That sackful of pistols turned out to be what got me to Paris at the end of the war. Mack Jones, our executive officer, and I didn't want to take that forty-and-eight boxcar train ride back to Paris, so we went to Paderborn, Germany, where there was an airstrip and the wounded were being flown out of there back to England. Some C-47s came in to pick up the wounded. I went up to the major who was in command of the flight and opened up my ditty bag, showing him all those German pistols. I told him to take his pick, but then he'd have to drop us off in Paris. He grabbed one of those pistols and told me they'd have to be back by five o'clock or get shot down. I told him that was his worry, just get us to Paris. When we got on that C-47, it was like a bus. There were wounded stacked along the sides. We had to stand up in there holding onto a strap like you would on a city bus, all the way to Paris. He dumped us at the airfield and almost ran us over trying to get out of there so fast. The plane barely stopped before we were off it. He was in such a hurry to get back to England.

So, Mack Jones and I were in Paris in late April when Roosevelt died. The French people were all crying. They worshipped Roosevelt. We were in Paderborn, Germany, on V-E Day, which was May 8, 1945.

After the war, I ended up in Heidelburg. We had a lot of general prisoners who had been court-martialed for things like murder. Some were under death sentence. So, we were delegated as constabulary to guard these prisoners. I had ninety-six points which would let me come home, but they wouldn't let me because they needed a medical officer for every thousand men. We had over seven hundred men. Fifth Army Headquarters was in Heidelburg then, and Mack Jones got transferred to there. We were close friends, so Mack had a plan to get me out of there. He got my rank changed from medical, and within a matter of hours, I was in a Jeep on my way to Reims. We hung around there for a long time, then they put us on trucks to Marseilles. That was a long truck ride. I was now in the 744th Light Tank Battalion. We nicknamed that battalion the 744th Light "Dog" Battalion. These guys had collected a bunch of dogs as pets and were determined to take them back home with them to the States. The ship we were going home on was delayed for one month. Finally, we boarded. The Transportation Corps Officer immediately named me as medical officer for the trip home. Right behind me came a whole hospital group which had been in India. There were majors, lieutenant colonels, and everything. But I'd already been named the Commanding Medical Officer. This meant I got to eat top side with the captain.

There was always a big craps game going on the ship. Enlisted men were the best craps shooters in the world! On payday, they always got in a big craps game until one person won all the money, which was in money orders. It was part of the way they survived. Three soldiers came to me during sick-call. One of them wanted to take a shower. He told me he had a money belt on which contained $ 150,000.00 in money orders which he'd won shooting craps, and that the two guys with him were his body guards. He told me he was paying them each $ 2,500.00 to guard him. He was afraid someone was going to steal the money orders and push him overboard. But he made it home and got off the ship with his money orders in tact.

Lal Duncan Threlkeld

We were twelve hundred men overloaded. This meant they had to sleep in shifts. It took eleven days to get to Hampton Roads, Virginia, where we had to go through quarantine. As the medical officer, I had to declare we had no contagious diseases. And I knew about all the dogs. They'd brought them on the ship in their duffel bags. That ship was just running with dogs, probably about forty. I went around to these guys and told them we were getting ready to dock soon. I told them they weren't allowed to have any type of wildlife, including dogs, and if I saw any of them leaving with a dog, I would kill them personally. I was ready to get home! I remember one old boy coming down the gang plank with a German Shepherd in his duffel bag. That duffel bag was waggling all around. He looked at me, and I looked at him. Nobody said a word.

As we crossed the Atlantic on our way home, we talked about how long it would take the bastards to start another war. And they did- Korea in 1950; then Viet Nam; and recently, Desert Storm. They know how to dream them up.

In 1944, I went, I did my job, and that was it. I returned home and met my eighteen-month-old daughter in November 1945. I resumed my residency in gynecology at Syracuse and finished in 1947. My wife and I had three more children, and now we have three grandchildren. I enjoyed a forty-year practice in my specialty in Oklahoma City, retiring in 1988. It's been a great life!

Chapter Twenty-two

Jack M. Williams

December 4, 1998

My background is a little different because I was raised in a foster family. I was born June 17, 1921, near Scranton, Pennsylvania, to a coal mining family of Welsh descent. When my father could not take care of my older sister and me after my mother's death in 1928, I went to stay with the Wright family in New Jersey for two weeks. I was nine years old at the time, and ended up staying until I was grown. If the Wrights had not kept me, I would have been sent to work in the coal mines. Before Mother Wright died, she told me how I came to stay on with them. She said I came to her and said I wanted to stay, and that if they kept me, I would make good. That was a nine-year-old's promise, and I'm still working on it.

I was a student at Rutgers University when Pearl Harbor was attacked. On December 7, 1941, I was in New York City with a friend attending a Giants/Dodgers professional football game. All during the game, we heard over the loud speakers for various colonels to report to their regiments. We didn't know what was going on. When we came out, we saw huge headlines on the newspapers that said, "Pearl Harbor Bombed." We said at that point that we probably weren't going to have much of a future in college. I decided to take flying during the second semester that year, which really was kind of dumb, knowing that the service would want to take anybody who could fly an airplane. Once I got my pilot's license, I was told I could either go in the army or the navy. I tried the army, but I was too small.

My flight instructor was a Polish cop and in the Naval Reserve. He swore like something I never heard in my life. Unbelievable. And I put him in positions where he had to swear. He encouraged me to get in the navy. So, I went to the Cadet Selection Board in New York City. After the physical examination, I was told my blood pressure was too low to get in the navy. I was told to go home, eat raw liver, and return in two weeks. When I came back, my blood pressure was still down. At this point, a corpsman said to me, "You really want to get in the navy?" He told me to go out for lunch at a bar, and after eating, drink a couple shots of bourbon. Now, I was a student with no money for this sort of thing. But I did as he suggested. I wandered back to the selection board after lunch. A different doctor was on duty for the afternoon examinations. I went through the line, and this time my blood pressure was perfect. I was passed through. But, really, I shouldn't have ever gotten in the navy at all!

I entered a preliminary training program. The navy did not have an organized program at that time for recruiting and training. I was sent to Rensselaer Institute in lower New York state. There, we had ground school, and practice flying. Our uniform was U.S. Navy khakis with U.S. Army Air Corps caps. Everything was all mixed up.

After two months, I went to preflight school in Chapel Hill, North Carolina. When we arrived, we were met at the bus by the Rutgers University football coach and his staff. They had been assigned to run this preflight school. Here, they would work on changing us from being noncombatant, softy types to tough guys. We were just a whole bunch of nice college kids who had to be made into men in a hurry. We ran obstacle courses and were taught not to stop and help others. We were made to box with our roommate until one of us was bleeding.

Three weeks before I arrived at Chapel Hill, George W. Bush began his training there. President Bush received his wings three weeks before me in Corpus Christi, Texas. We never met each other during that time, but our navy careers were on the same track.

Then the navy shipped me to Norman, Oklahoma. There I flew Yellow Perils. I found out that Oklahoma was the only place you could stand in mud up to your knees and have dry sand blow in your face. On our first liberty, a friend and I took the Interurban Trolley in to Oklahoma City from Norman. And that's how I met and married Margaret, who was from Altus, Oklahoma. She and her friend were attending a dance for the air corps men at The

Biltmore Hotel. We persuaded them to get us into the dance, each pair of friends planning to ditch the other pair once inside. But it didn't work out that way. I spent the entire evening teaching Margaret how to jitterbug and dance like we did back east. We eventually married in Coronado, California, in December 1943.

After receiving my Naval Aviator Wings on July 1, 1943, I went to Fort Lauderdale, Florida, for torpedo bomber training. Then I went up to the Great Lakes to qualify on a little converted ferry boat which was supposed to be like a carrier deck. We practiced our take-offs and landings on Lake Michigan, and then left to join Torpedo Squadron Twenty-one in San Diego.

Six weeks after getting married, my name was drawn from a hat along with four other names of naval aviators to leave the next day in preparation for the Marshall Islands invasion. I received orders to go to San Francisco for transportation on a Jeep carrier holding about three hundred pilots in anticipation of many casualties from the impending Marshall Islands invasion. Among the five of us traveling to San Francisco together was one wild pilot who was a great poker player. He also knitted. He actually knitted. And he knitted on the train all the way up to San Francisco. He just knitted right along. It quite unnerved the whole train, I think. He managed to get himself killed in Guam by making a second run for a photographer to get pictures. That's when they got him.

Margaret made the ride with me up to San Francisco, and we stayed at a hotel. The rest of the men went elsewhere together. Although all our orders were for a 2400 (midnight) check-in, it was a mistake and should have been 1200 (noon). The rest of the group found out about it, and got in with the four hundred men leaving immediately. I didn't make it. When I showed up, they said I would get air transportation out of there. They put me on a China Clipper, a big flying boat with four big engines on it. The U.S. Navy had taken this over from Pan American to use for taking out marine generals, admirals, and navy captains. Nobody like me, an ensign, the lowest rank, would be on this craft. I didn't even know anything about protocol; how to act around all these high-ranking officers. But I left with them from Treasure Island, between San Francisco and Oakland. It was luxurious, complete with sterling silver service, plush sofas and easy chairs, and mounds of fresh fruit displayed. We almost ran through a destroyer taking off. I watched a marine general's face turn white as a sheet as we went under the Oakland Bay Bridge narrowly missing that destroyer. I thought we were going to hit it, too, but we managed to avoid it. We were headed to the Pacific. A navy captain befriended me and helped me find my way around. Meanwhile, those other four hundred navy pilots were out at sea rocking around on that small carrier, getting deathly sick. I arrived ahead of them. The day before I got there, the fleet had already left for the Marshall Islands, and all four hundred of us missed getting to go out!

I was assigned to Torpedo Squadron VT One. The planes we flew were called Avengers. There were three men to a crew: the pilot, turret gunner, and the radio man down below. The pilot was totally isolated from the other two crew members.

We resumed training on Oahu, Hawaii, in January 1944. In May, we were assigned to the USS Yorktown, also called "The Fighting Lady." This was just in time for the Marianas operations. Our job as pilots was to go in and bomb the runways and anything else that would interfere with the landings of the Marines on these islands. The night before Guam, I couldn't eat, I couldn't sleep. As soon as we were up circling, I got dry heaves, and I couldn't throw up. Hell, I was trying to do everything I could because I was just sick. I was scared. I was scared to death. I was gonna get killed. Then as soon as we got signaled to break off and start going on targets, we knew where we were going, and after that I was all right. I didn't have any problems at all. When I saw a burst of antiaircraft fire, I would turn right into it figuring a guy wouldn't shoot twice in the same place. It became my challenge to do the job, to get down and drop my bombs, to get back and rendezvous, and get back on the ship. I was not the risk-taking type.

We made two runs a day. When we made the early morning run, we got up at four o'clock and took off while it was still dark. We were part of the Marianas Turkey Shoot which was between the Japanese Navy and the U.S. Navy. Our fighters shot down hundreds and hundreds of Japanese fighters.

When someone today says they don't see how I was able to land my plane on a carrier, I say, "I don't know either." Because I really don't know. When I look at some of the pictures, I wonder how in the world it could have been. Of course, the answer is that we were trained to do it. Nobody ever told us we couldn't do it. So, we just did it.

The flight deck on our carrier was about six hundred feet long. We didn't land at an angle like nowadays, but straight ahead. Seventy-five feet above the water, the landing deck was a moving target as the waves rocked the ship back and forth, and up and down. There was a signal officer on deck giving the pilot directions for landing. A tail hook on the plane would catch one of six hydraulic cables which were stretched across the deck, allowing the plane to slow down. After the plane stopped, it was rolled back to disengage the tail hook from the cable. Then the wings folded down, like a bird, and the plane was parked on the deck. Also, there was a wire or mesh barrier about five feet high which would stop a plane in case its tail hook didn't catch a cable. In over sixty landings I made, I never hit a barrier and I never got hurt. I never had to belly land or bail out. Once we landed a little hard and broke off a tail wheel. Another time we nearly ran out of gas and had just enough to get back on the deck when the engine quit. We must have had our gas line hit one time because we started to get gas fumes through the plane. We could have put on our oxygen masks, but we would have run out of oxygen before we got back. The decision was made to split the gas and oxygen half and half until we could get back. We were sick as dogs for three days after we got back, having inhaled all those gas fumes.

The deck was spotted with three different types of planes, about fifty total. The dive bombers were last, then the torpedo bombers, and the fighters were up in front because they didn't need as much runway to get off the deck. Sometimes catapults were used for take-offs. You'd have to harness in for the catapult. The force was so strong that it put you out of control momentarily. Since the pilots were also the navigators, it was important to have the settings so the plane could operate correctly until the pilot regained control. I was short in stature, and this force always made my feet come off the controls. There was nothing I could do to stop it. Once I got going, I was all right.

Sometimes there were as many as three or four carriers together. When all the planes were in the air that would be nearly three hundred planes. Sometimes there was only two hundred feet before we were in the clouds, and when we got over the clouds, we couldn't see where we had been. Then there was the problem of coming back and finding where we needed to land. Our carrier would move to another location while we were gone. Perhaps it would move into a rain squall to hide from the enemy. If we came back to find our carrier gone, we had to do a square search until we picked up a signal. Each ship had its own identifying radio signal, or homing signal, which only we could pick up. That's how we would find our way back to the ship. We were usually away from the ship about three or four hours. On return, if there were no crashes on deck and everything went smoothly, we could land a plane every two or three minutes.

One type of bombing we did was called glide bombing. The dive bombers went straight down, but the glide bombers went at a forty-five degree angle. The bombs were dropped at about eight hundred feet. Sometimes we did skip bombing where we dropped a 500-pound bomb at about two hundred feet. The bomb would hit the ground and bounce up into the freighter and explode. We carried up to two thousand pounds in bombs on one plane. Or we could carry a torpedo. But in our environment, at that point in the war, we really didn't do anything with torpedoes.

* * *

In the summer of 1945, we were operating off the USS Bennington. It was our mission to operate over Japan, making strikes against cities, and dropping bombs in the Inland Sea. Later on, we had instructions that if Hiroshima was obscured, we were to pick an alternate target. What we didn't know is that they had already picked the site where the atomic bomb would be dropped.

I went on a rescue mission. My job was to find someone who might be down in Japan's inland sea and drop an eight-man life raft from my bomb bay to give a better chance of survival. I saw a fighter pilot down. He was keeping afloat on his one-man raft, paddling like mad trying to get out of there. I called in a rescue submarine. I used a light to send him instructions about which way to head. He was being shot at from the shore. This complicated my approach to drop the raft to him. We came in from behind him and dropped the raft from about fifty feet, then the turret gunner and I both strafed the shoreline with our 50-caliber machine guns as we turned to get out of there. It was getting late and we had to get back. Gas was low. I found the carrier and was signaled in, only to find out it was the wrong one! It turned out to be the USS Hancock. We were just glad someone didn't come up and say, "Ah, so!" Just after landing, we came under kamikaze attack, so we spent the night there. The next morning we were launched by catapult and made it back to the correct carrier.

When we were on the USS Bennington, it was toward the end of the war. Many of our capital ships had been hit by kamikazes. So, they began to use destroyer escorts or pickets. They put these pickets out about fifty miles from our carrier task force consisting of carriers, cruisers, battleships, and other support ships. These manned destroyer pickets determined entrance to the area. When we left on a mission, we had a certain sector for re-entry upon our return. If we tried to come in at a different sector other than the one assigned us, the picket would shoot at us. He might not hit us, but it reminded us we were at the wrong sector. There were instances where our own fighter pilots were shot down by the destroyers because they kept coming after the initial warning. There was too much at stake to make assumptions. Keep in mind, the sectors changed every twenty minutes. I can remember being a couple of minutes off and thinking, "Oops! Wrong door! Let's go find another one where we're supposed to be!"

At the end of the war, we were dropping bombs on a radar plant in the heart of Tokyo. Everyday. We were dropping them from eight hundred feet, right down on top of the buildings practically. We were getting ready to make another strike, and we had about three hundred planes flying at twelve thousand feet. Just as we got over Tokyo Bay, they radioed and said, "Jettison your bombs. Return to base." The atomic bomb had been dropped on Hiroshima. The war was over. But we didn't know that at the time. We turned around, and I said to the crew, "Get behind the armor plate, we're going home." We jettisoned our bombs into the ocean. I looked out the back of the plane and saw fighter planes celebrating, doing all kinds of wild aerobatics. A few of them got picked off by the Japanese. As far as the Japanese were concerned at that point, it wasn't over.

When the surrender was signed on the USS Missouri, our group and squadron were pictured flying over it with a thousand planes. We were the number one squadron on the right hand side, the lead planes. That was a nice experience to have.

After the war, we had the job of finding prisoner of war camps in Japan. Usually, those were placed at the base of a mountain so they could keep the prisoners busy working in mines. When we found one, we would fly supplies in to them. We would drop down packages which floated down on little parachutes. They contained food, clothing, and first aid supplies. Some of the packages landed outside the area, and the Japanese began to pick them up. After that, we brought along our fighter planes to strafe along the sides to discourage the Japanese from going after the packages. One of the last times that we went in, I decided I wanted to send a message to the prisoners. I wrote on a piece of paper, "To all you wonderful allies and G.I.s... glad that we're here...." and I included the names and addresses of me and my crew. I put it in a message drop, which has a sand bag to give it weight, and I threw it over the side. That Christmas I got letters and cards from men who got my message. One was a medical corps lieutenant colonel from Whitehall, London, England; another was from Brooklyn, New York. I thought that was the best part of the war because I was doing something to help somebody.

* * *

Some men are uncomfortable talking about their war experiences. It depends on where you were. The airmen's world was more contained, a little smaller. We were treated well. We died fast, but we didn't suffer. We were scared, yes, all the darned time, but it got to be a competition between me and the other guy. It was different being in the air as opposed to on the ground in a trench somewhere, or in a tank.

Our inner feelings are best conveyed by what we do, and not what we say. That's probably how I got in the service. I was needed. I wasn't thinking about what I was doing, just doing what was needed. That was a form of patriotism. I get uncomfortable when somebody talks down America, or burns or desecrates the American flag. I think a person should support his country, work for his country, honor his country and those who have gone before. I feel that very strongly. I believe that anything you believe in, you have to show some energy to support it. We need to be strong Americans; stand up for what we believe in. I hope that it means something to my children that I served my country. In our family, growing up, it was important that you were loyal to your country and your flag. We celebrated the Fourth of July, and on Decorations Day we decorated the cemeteries. We learned a lot of American history growing up on the east coast.

I'm more a feeling person than a fact person. I'm not the mechanical type. I do a lot of things from my heart. I was always very sensitive to burials at sea. Sometimes we lost a whole crew. Hardly a day went by that there wasn't a service. Everybody went. The body was put in a shroud with weights applied, and then slid off the side into the sea. I attended almost all those services. And I attended the religious services held on the ship. I suspect that part of my immature faith was there at the time, and that it helped me. I know I asked for a lot of help. I still ask for a lot of help, more now than I did then.

My nature is to help someone, not take advantage or hurt. I never wanted to be involved with anything that would hurt somebody. I am more concerned for others than for myself.

I plan on everything going smoothly, but I prepare for the worst. I'm not a worrier, just a planner. In the navy, I learned defensive flying, to expect the worst so that I could handle emergencies. No surprises. That's how to stay in control of what you're trying to get done. That kind of help can't hurt you.

One way I've lived my life is to keep out of trouble. That came from being raised in a foster home. I wouldn't have gotten to stay with them if I hadn't learned to keep out of trouble. It was like an axe over my head that I was there subject to good behavior.

My foster family had a summer home on the coast of New Jersey where we spent six hours a day in the ocean. I still love the water, and I have a sail boat. One of my attitudes about life is, "If I were drowning, I would like to be trying not to the last time I go down." Never give up. Absolutely, don't ever give up. As long as I can survive a situation, that's fine; it doesn't bother me. The fact that I went through it is not as important as where I ended up.

My foster father, Pop Wright, was a golfer. He always said to me, "Never up, never in," and, "Always aim for the hole." It was his way of saying to make the full effort.

* * *

I came to live in Oklahoma in 1952. The insurance business was suggested to me, and I ended up going with New York Life. I didn't know anybody; started from scratch. I've been at it for forty-seven years. All the friends I have are clients in insurance. That's the reason I can never retire. I've got to be around as long as they need me. I try to stay active, exercise, eat right, and keep my brain going. Staying on top of my life insurance business and all that goes along with it, keeps me on the ball. I want to go on working as long as I can.

One thing I love to do is play the piano. I play for the enjoyment of it. As a child in the foster home where I grew up, I began playing "My Country 'Tis of Thee" on the piano just from having heard it on the radio. I found out later that my biological mother had played the piano, but I didn't know it as a

Jack M. Williams

child. My enjoyment of playing the piano comes from the enjoyment received by the listener. That's what motivates me.

My personality requires that I do something for somebody else. If I were not in the life insurance business, I'm sure I would have been in the ministry because I feel I have to pay something back. My greatest thrill is doing something for somebody else. I want to be remembered as a man who encouraged others, somewhere along the line, to make their lives better.

CHAPTER TWENTY-THREE

CLEO M. WILLOUGHBY

JULY 11, 1998

As a young man, I worked breaking in horses on my friend's family ranch of ten thousand acres in Pawhuska, Oklahoma. There weren't many jobs available during The Depression.

In 1935, I enlisted in the United States Army, Forty-fifth Division, because I needed the money to go to college. I got twelve dollars every three months for my enrollment fee. I was totally unaware and uninformed about the conflicts overseas in 1939.

I went to the National Guard summer camp in 1940. We were mobilized to Fort Sill, Oklahoma, in September of that year. I did not have to go to World War II because I was married and in college, but I went for my hometown and to get in with people I knew to "get my years in." It took me almost six years to get out.

We were poorly informed about the international situation. It was in December 1941 when Pearl Harbor was bombed that we became aware of hostilities going on other than in Germany.

I knew by 1943 that my life would be impacted. Until then I was only "in training." I had been in active duty for over a year when Pearl Harbor was bombed. I thought we would be sent right on after Pearl Harbor, but we were not.

I was afraid to go, but had a lot of respect for what was going on. I was twenty-six years old, a little older than a lot of the men I was associated with at that time. Because I was married and had a baby daughter, I naturally had certain reservations about what was going on. But the old saying is, "I was shot in the rear with an American Flag." I had a job to do and somebody had to do it. That's the attitude you develop.

We went to Tiverton, England in April 1944. We went over on the Queen Elizabeth. That was pretty good! The soldiers took turns with sleeping arrangements. We would sleep on deck one night, then down below the next night.

In England, I trained with the Fourth Infantry Division for fire support. We had a company attached to each of the assault battalions for Utah Beach. We were attached to the Third Battalion, Twenty-second Infantry, Fourth Division of the First Army. We trained for about four weeks. We were housed in civilian housing because the fields were so full, so help me, with ammunition, equipment, and Americans. I stayed with the postmaster in Tiverton. Supplies which the United States had been sending over for years in preparation were stacked up everywhere, all along the roadsides.

We were unaware that our unit was scheduled for the assault landing at Utah Beach on D-Day. After boarding the ships, we were briefed in detail on the landing operations and we were informed as to how lucky we were to be a part of the largest show on earth!

We went from Tiverton to Normandy on a troop ship which was part of a fleet of five thousand. Three of the troop ships were directed to Utah Beach. One was assault force; one was backup. I was on the assault troop ship. The sea was really rough, the roughest they'd had. We lost many men trying to transfer from the large ships to the smaller crafts which would take us further inland. The men had to go down a rope and swing out to the smaller boat. Some were crushed between the two crafts. The waves were so terrific that the small boats would bounce off the large ship and men would either fall between the boats and get crushed or fall into the water with all their heavy equipment on their backs. There were about forty people with mortar on their backs. I had one boat and my platoon sergeant had the other boat. The casualties had begun before we even began to fight. I knew I had to make it into the smaller boat and I knew I would just do it. My platoon sergeant and I were told we were in charge of the smaller boats.

We circled for a long time in the smaller boat, waiting. The air force started their operation at midnight. They pulled gliders over us the next morning with the CO C-47s in front. They were pretty ineffective. They had many casualties on the landings. And the Germans had anti-invasion poles set up in these fields which would knock the wings off the gliders and wreck them. They knew we had gliders.

We could see the skyline light up. I was thinking I was about to get killed. I was thinking, "Here we are. This is it." This was the first time we had seen any real armed conflict. It didn't look good, really.

The navy had come across from England following the big ships and the smaller boats which were called LCMs. On the LCM, the front goes down and you walk out. They told us there were sand bars out quite a ways from the beach. The tendency was to hit one of those and then you couldn't go any further. Then you jump off and you go out of sight. And you drown. You were carrying a rifle along with the equipment on your back which was hard to swim with and would force you down.

Sure enough we hit a sand bar. And it was as far from the sand bar to the beach as two football fields. The sailor driving the LCM said, "This is as far as I can go." And I said, "Now, wait a minute. This is a long ways from the beach." We weren't taking fire anyway. I told him, "I'm in charge of this and if you don't back this sucker up to try it again, I'm gonna kill ya. I've got forty men in here who I don't want to die for lack of effort on your part." He backed up, hit another one, and it shuddered a little. And he went on over it. When we got out the water was only about knee deep. So we made it to the beach and did not incur any casualties until later. We hit the beach about four o'clock in the morning, June 6, 1944. The weather was mild. Then it got real bloody.

We had never even fired over anyone's head until we got to Utah Beach. They pulled us a little green and we were a little reluctant to do these things.

When we got on the beach we set up a platoon installation so we could start firing. Ahead of us was an observer. He'd find the targets and send back the coordinates by radio. There were three radios in our company. I picked out a depressed spot on the beach, a hole so we wouldn't get direct artillery or fire on us. That worked, but we got bombed by four P-47s from our own side. Fortunately, no one was killed, but the sand caved in on one fellow, and we ran and dug him out. He was all right.

Our job was to go up the beach line with the battalion that I was supporting and clean out these big concrete emplacements on the right flank. Two other battalions went on in. Then my battalion went on into Normandy, and suffered, oh Lord, lots of casualties.

The bravest people that I know were the boys who took off from behind the sea wall and deliberately ran through mine fields to clear it for others to follow. You'd see a leg fly, then an arm fly. Their attitude was, "We gotta go. We can't win this thing standing here on the beach." We thought: There he goes flying, and there he lays dying. That took a lot of guts from those kids. A lot of determination. A lot of leadership. You have to think about how many of them did it. We'd landed about one-fourth mile from where we were supposed to and that complicated things for a while. All the sand dunes were full of mines

I went up to the other platoon to look for another location. There was a farmhouse with a courtyard around it, like they have in Europe. We were just getting in there, when the U.S. Navy hit us. They killed three people and set the weapons carrier that had ammunition on it afire.

We ran through the German Achtung mine fields in the alfalfa planted on the low grounds. Behind the beach and the sand dunes, the Germans had flooded a lot of it to make another hazard. It was waist-deep water. There were only one or two roads across that. A lot of air force men who'd been killed were lying in the water, and they were up in the trees. This was the first time we'd seen anything like it. We began to realize we were into a really hard war against a well-trained enemy. The Germans were an ingenious people. Technologically, their weapons and their equipment were so far ahead of us it was pathetic. Although we had a lot of equipment, theirs was better. For instance, their automatic weapons were light and air-cooled, and ours were heavy and water-cooled, not very mobile. They were a well-disciplined organization. I was beginning to think I was on "the wrong side."

The only thing that saw me through any of this was the will to live. I prayed. As they say, "There was never an atheist in a foxhole." I'd never smoked a cigarette until I got into Normandy and was down in the foxhole. They'd given us each two packs of cigarettes. That night, when I was scared, I put a poncho over my head and lit up a cigarette. It was something different. Something to do.

When we got inland, we saw hedgerows where many casualties had occurred. These hedgerows were formed from field clearing. They were as high as five feet and even had trees growing in them. They served as a natural defense line depending on which side you were on. We saw paratroopers who had been dropped and hit heavily by German antiaircraft. When they landed, they had scattered widely and were not able to provide efficient maneuvering until they could regroup to make a forceful unit and get reorganized. Those units were collected and made into an assault force for the first objective, Saint Mere-Eglise, after securing the beaches. After that, we took Monteburg, a small town en route to Valognes. We had a difficult time and suffered more heavy casualties.

We were trying to cut the peninsula off at the port of Cherbourg. The Germans had filled it up with ships that they sunk in order to block the port facilities. After landing on the beach, we had to walk over a hundred miles to get to Cherbourg. As the platoon leader I got to ride in a Jeep most of the time.

Our only shelter was the foxholes. When we got into towns where there might be buildings, they were mostly burned out and bombed out. The supplies they gave us for the initial invasion included a small package of dehydrated food. It was called K-rations. We had that for ten days. Then we got the C-rations which was the canned food and crackers and such. This was from the company supply outfit. The quarter master built up on the beaches. Then the unit went back to establish contact and tell the company's location so they could bring them supplies.

Our biggest problem was that there were no forward air controllers with the tactical units. We were fighting and trying to advance and move. By the time an air strike was called back to England, the ground forces might have moved a ways. And by the time the American bombers arrived, their own ground forces might seem the target as they were moving. The bombers could only drop the bombs where they were supposed to drop them. There was no one to call it off, to halt the mission. The shortcoming of the army air force was no forward air control.

This is what happened on the St. Lo-Perrier Road: The American bombers dropped the bombs as far back as fifteen miles from the targets. They killed Americans in division headquarters. Why? Because where we evacuated, there were these foxholes on a certain side of the road. Our air force, P-47s and tactical air craft, were supposed to strafe some bombs in that area after our evacuation. Then the median bombers were supposed to hit behind the road to take out their support units. The Liberators and Flying Fortresses were to hit behind where the German artillery was- deeper back. The bomb release point was the road, but over time, the wind changed. It created a dust line. The dust line came back over us. The road could not be seen by the bombers. So the dust line, where we were, became the bomb release point. And they killed a lot of Americans.

Frequently, it's said that the "Great" Patton and his Third Army effected the break-through out of Normandy. His army was behind the First Army awaiting the break-out. He exploited the First Army's break-out with his heavily armored units. The flamboyant General Patton was called "Old Blood and Guts," but it was our blood, and his guts.

Then I was in the Battle of the Bulge. We had a lot of casualties. I arrived right after Malmedy where one hundred-twenty five Americans were executed. The Battle of the Bulge was Germany's last big offensive. Our own intelligence was terrible. They didn't even know this was going to happen. You'd think with the Germans moving all those Tiger tanks around, our intelligence would have known it. But they didn't. We were deployed on Christmas Day 1944. We had Christmas dinner en route in a field. The Germans had dressed in U.S. uniforms and changed the road signs to add to the confusion. The weather was terrible- extremely cold and foggy. This made our air support ineffective. After the Battle of the Bulge, Germany was strictly retaliatory.

I was at Kaiserslautern, the German spy depot, where the our air force caught the Germans evacuating and there was a mass slaughter. Bodies of men and horses had to be pushed off the road by a bulldozer.

We crossed the Rhine River at Worms. We got up to the foot hills of the Bavarian Mountains and we released the Russian POW hospital, which was an unsightly task. We released those who were able to walk and evacuated most of the others.

Then we were at one of the concentration camps which had killed the Jews. The sign in front said, "Enter through here and leave through the smoke stacks." The people in the little town said they didn't know what was going on there. But they were lying. They had to know it was going on. The dead bodies were stacked like cordwood. We made the Germans still there crawl across the corpses. The Jewish people who remained alive were severely emaciated.

I never felt safe until we were in Leipzig and I knew I was on my way home. All resistance had stopped except on the eastern front where the Russians were assaulting Berlin. War is hell. It sure is.

After I was discharged, I came home. I came back on the Queen Mary and arrived in New York City. The Statue of Liberty looked very good. But I was upset and tense. I was straight out of combat. I couldn't sleep. There were a lot of psychological problems. You have to rehabilitate yourself to a civilian type of life. I didn't know whether I would or not. I'd get up in the morning and go hide in the woods, tell them I was squirrel hunting. It takes time to wipe these things out when you've incurred things like having blood splashed on you from a friend.

There was that time I was standing in a German courtyard and an artillery shell came in and it killed three of my men... I was standing right there with them... I never got even a touch. Makes you think, "WHY?"

And one of the worst things about being in combat is you take a young group of people with you, nineteen, twenty, twenty-one years old. You come back, they look forty .... from the mental torture and anguish and the, "Why me, Lord? Why should I have to go?"

In the infantry, it's unfortunate, but this is fact: there is no relief for an infantryman unless he gets killed, or unless he gets what's called the million-dollar wound, for which he would be evacuated. The most an infantryman can hope for is reorganization, or replacement of lost men. I've actually seen in foxholes, when the artillery barrage came in, feet and arms sticking up out of the foxholes, hoping to get that million-dollar wound. Anything to get out.

On August 6, 1945, I was on leave with my family in Muskogee, Oklahoma. We heard the news of Hiroshima. We went downtown where people were drinking alcohol, dancing, kissing, and celebrating with firecrackers. We decided to go home when someone threw a firecracker in our car.

I thought it was over but I had to go to Korea in 1951 and go through more of the same thing. I was with the same unit. It was a different type of war, but the same in some ways. I went over there as a First Lieutenant and came back as a Major in a year's time. Not because I was good. I just out-lived everyone.

General Van Fleet was one of the people I admired greatly. He became the Commanding General in Korea. Also, I admired General Wyrick. He was highly decorated and a person I had a great deal of respect for. I admired his bravery, intelligence, camaraderie, and his love of family. He was a "number one" guy. He later became the Commanding General in Viet Nam.

Cleo M. Willoughby

Patriotism, in my estimation, is the loyalty and the determination to see that this great country will prevail over all else. And I think we are privileged to have lived in it during this period. We have seen it develop from the wagon period to rocket ships going to the moon. I'd say, during World War II, this country probably became the world leader when we really weren't ready for it.

The young people today don't have much respect for old people to tell them things. So, you're better off, if you're not intimately related, to leave them alone. They think, "He's old. He doesn't know any better." But I did tell my grandson in a letter I wrote when he was a week old that you have to start to develop lines of communication sometime. That's what makes the world go around: communication.

What I would tell someone is, "Let's get together, get our heads on right, and make this country bigger, better, and more beautiful." I think we're negligent in taking care of what we have. It wouldn't hurt each and every one of the young people today to go overseas and see how they take care of their countries.

I got nine battle stars. Five were from Europe; four from Korea. But I was not a hero. I wouldn't change anything about my life if I had it to live over, but I might like to get a little better educated. I've been reluctant, at my age, to change with the tide as far as modern communications, like computers.

I feel fortunate to even be here after World War II. I've never been in contact with anyone I was on the Normandy beach with. One thing about front line troops, the grime and the dirt, the unpredictability of life itself... it was one of the greatest examples of camaraderie that you'll ever see. We took care of each other. And that's distinctive about the American people. We had to rely on each other. We were like family.

I want to be remembered as a decent father. After all, it's my family who's important. And I cherish them very much.

CHAPTER TWENTY-FOUR

DORRIS WELLS WILSON

DECEMBER 1998

I was born in Stephens, Arkansas, on October 6, 1926. Mine was a large Methodist family. I lived right across the street from my good friend, Morgan Moore, and I wouldn't be doing this interview if not for him!

Two weeks before I was eighteen years old, I began to beg my mother to sign papers so I could go in the navy. She didn't want to, but finally she did. I hadn't finished high school, and I had to quit in order to go in the service. Guy Smith, Jr., my friend, had already finished high school and was going in, so we both went in the service together. We left Little Rock on September 23, 1944, and went to San Diego for our training. We had ten weeks of hard boot training. Everything in boot camp was timed. We went to bed at a certain time; had to get up at a certain time; eat at a certain time; smoke at a certain time....Those ten weeks were hard, but we made it. After that, we got a ten-day leave to come home.

Three days after returning from leave, my division got orders to go aboard the USS Franklin, "Big Ben," in Bremerton, Washington. Over three hundred of us left San Diego for Washington on a troop train. It took us three days to get there, arriving on Christmas Day 1944. When we went aboard the ship, everything was iced up and snowed up.

Our division was to be replacements for the men who had been killed on the USS Franklin at the Battle of Leyte Gulf. I was put into the Second Gunnery Division. We left Washington on January 31, 1945, for Alameda,

California, to pick up our planes. It took three days to get there and I was seasick the whole three days. I well remember when we went under the Golden Gate Bridge in San Francisco.

We picked up a hundred U.S. Marine pilots and a hundred planes, Air Group Five, and headed toward Hawaii. As we headed toward Hawaii, we maneuvered, allowing these pilots to practice taking off and landing on a carrier. None of them were used to this. I would sit up there on the island structure, watching these planes take off and land. The air would catch some of them and throw them back, some would burst on landing, and some would miss and go over the drink. We lost several men that way between Alameda and Hawaii. We buried one at sea.

When we got to Pearl Harbor, Hawaii, on February 12, they gave us all liberty. I went into town and was promptly picked up by the Military Police for jay-walking. I was given a ticket to go back to the ship. Dumb me, I did. I got laughed at for that. If I'd known then what I know now, I wouldn't have ever gone back to that ship.

On March 3, we headed for the war zone, arriving on March 13 at Ulithi Lagoon. We prepared for action. I didn't know it at the time, but the USS Franklin was going to be the flagship for Task Force Fifty-eight. Vice Admiral Marc A. Mitscher was in command; Rear Admiral Ralph Davison was aboard the USS Franklin. We were fifty miles off the shore of Japan, and we were to strike the home islands of the Japanese Empire for the first time. It seemed like they had every ship in the navy over there at the time. This was the most powerful armada of warships in history. We were making air raids on Kyushu and Kobe, and preparing for invasion.

At seven o'clock in the morning on March 19, 1945, we got hit by two 500-pound bombs from the a Jap flying a twin-engined Judy. He was only fifty feet above deck. A lot of people said it was a kamikaze, but it wasn't.

I went to eat breakfast at six o'clock that morning. As I went to get in the chow line, I ran into one of my buddies and I broke line. I cheated that morning. I went on through the chow line and got breakfast. Just as I sat down, a bomb hit and exploded on the mess hall deck. Well, that bomb set off all our ammunitions and everything. That morning, all our planes were loaded and ready to go, and we had only about seven planes in the air when the first bomb hit. Within minutes, fire spread over the heavily armed planes, which set off a chain of terrific, violent explosions. The inferno was worsened by the detonations from the ammunition supplies, which were set off by other explosions. They estimated 62,000 pounds of ammunition on board; 30,000 gallons of jet fuel. This all exploded on the ship and did the damage. That's what tore us up. The second bomb struck aft, crashing through two decks and exploding on the third deck, near the chief petty officer's quarters.

We were all shoved into a compartment, about three hundred of us. All the hatches were knocked off. There was no way in the world we could get out. I was sitting on my buddy Allbright's lap because we were packed so tight in that compartment- three hundred men in a room about thirty feet square. It was dark and full of smoke. I couldn't see what was right in front of me. I remember telling him there was no way we were getting out of there. I told him we were going to die. We were in there for three hours. Dr. Jim Fuelling from Indiana was in there with us. He told us all to pray, to pray silent and not talk to one another, to save our energy. He prevented panic.

The smoke was so thick in that room, we could hardly breathe. It's a wonder we didn't all suffocate. We were below the waterline and there were no portholes. Our only air supply was through one six-inch hole. The ship had already listed about thirty-five degrees and we could hear all the explosions.

Lieutenant Donald A. Gary was in there with us, too. He knew the ship. He was on it the during its previous incident at Leyte. He told us he would find a way out, that he'd be back. He was gone about an hour. He crawled through the air ducts, wound around through those things, up five or six decks to the flight deck. This he did, blinded by thick smoke and surrounded by intense heat. He came back and told us, "Boys, I've found a way out, and what I want you to do is each one grab a shoulder, and we'll lead you out of here." And that's what we did. We crawled through the air ducts in chains of twenty up to the flight deck. Dr. Fuelling was the last man in the last group to escape our trap. When I hit that fresh air, it was heaven!

But I didn't know what to do then. Everything was just flames...flames going everywhere! The ship was a solid blaze. There wasn't much room to even maneuver around. So, I started running, and when I did, I felt explosions underneath me. I was blown up into the air, and I came down on my elbows. All I got was a scratch on one of my elbows. I saw a bunch of boys wrapped up in blankets. I got in a blanket, too, and just as I did, that's when we were attacked the second time. A Japanese plane came over and strafed us, strafed the whole deck. Bullets were just flying everywhere. I jumped up, threw the blanket off, and went to the farthest end of the ship I could go.

That's when I saw they were trying to get the tow line from the USS Pittsburgh to us. We were dead in the water and had been for several hours. The tow line was a six-inch steel cable. It had to be pulled a quarter of a mile from the USS Pittsburgh to us. We didn't have a thousand men to do it. We had about eighty men on that line. The colored boys began to holler, "Heave ho! Heave ho! Pull!" They were singing it. And they got that thing pulled up and tied onto our ship. That's when the USS Pittsburgh towed us out away from the war zone. The USS Santa Fe was circling us about three hundred feet out to protect us while we were doing all this.

After we got the tow line on, I came back to help on the fire line, whatever I could do. They hollered out from the bridge for anybody left from gunnery to come up and man the 40mm gun, the only gun on the whole ship still in operation. I went up there. I was first loader on the squad. Just as I got up there, I spotted a Japanese plane coming in, flying low. We turned the gun manually and started shooting. That sucker dropped that bomb and missed about six feet over the fan tail. After it was all over, we were given credit for saving the ship.

Admiral Davison wanted to sink the ship, abandon it, but Captain Leslie E. Gehres said no because there were men trapped below. He asked for air and surface support in order to save the USS Franklin. We started out with 3,200 men on board; 1,120 were killed. Some of the men were blown overboard, some jumped overboard, some got onto the USS Pittsburgh when it was along side us. When we got back to Pearl Harbor, the captain would not let those men return on the ship. He called them deserters because they abandoned ship.

* * *

We had a band director on the USS Franklin named H. K. "Saxie" Dowell. He wrote the popular song "Three Little Fishes." All the band instruments had been torn up, but he made instruments out of pots and pans, bottles and combs. And when we hit Hawaii, he began to play with this band. Seven hundred-four men sang this song written by our captain, to the tune of the "Marine Hymn." I'll sing it for you now:

From the Jap isle of Kyushu
To America's shining shore
We've brought our ship, the Franklin,
To be fixed to fight some more.
Oh, the Japs they thought they'd sunk us
As they came and came again.
But they couldn't get the shot in
That was marked to sink "Big Ben."
From the shores of Jap Kyushu,
By Ulithi's steaming strand,
And the isles of Aloha Nui,
We all come to our own land.
Many shipmates sail not with us,
But their spirit shall not die;
When our bugle sounds "To Stations,"
We will answer for them "Aye."

We returned to Ulithi, an island where ships went for small repairs. We were there for about five days getting our engines back in order. They finally got them where they would go about sixteen knots. Normal speed was about thirty-two knots.

We buried a lot of our dead there at Ulithi. They were buried like garbage. They had to be. Many of the dead were men from below who were so bloated in death that they could barely get them through the hatches. The smell was terrible. I couldn't go down there for three weeks. I stayed on the gun mount for three solid days with a life jacket around my waist. I slept up there on that steel deck, and ate up there, too.

After Ulithi, we got orders to go to Brooklyn Navy Yard. From Hawaii to New York, we came through the Panama Canal. The ship was so big it took us two days to get through there. The captain worked us four hours on, four hours off, for five straight weeks all the way back. We stripped that ship of everything, threw it over into the drink, the ocean. Everything, even airplane parts- there wasn't anything left on that ship when we got to Brooklyn Navy Yard. We cleaned that ship from one end to the other. We traveled thirteen

Dorris Wells Wilson

thousand miles from Kyushu to New York. Out of 3,200, we had 704 men who brought that ship back to the States. It was the most heavily damaged warship ever to reach port under her own power. Captain Gehres said, "A ship that *will* not be sunk, can not be sunk."

* * *

I remember a man named Fairchild, from Camden, Arkansas, came up to me on deck and said he recognized me from home. He told me he had a feeling he wasn't going to make it. He said if that happened he wanted me to get in touch with his mother. He was in the air division, and was killed. Just as soon as I could, after I got back home, I did find and visit his mother. After I got my discharge, I almost cracked up. But I got over it.

I weighed one hundred-twenty pounds when I got in the navy, and only ninety-eight pounds when I got home. I lost twenty-two pounds in five weeks. If I had it to do all over again, I wouldn't volunteer. Although I don't like the idea of war, I did my duty. I was responsible and I did my part, the best I could.

CHAPTER TWENTY-FIVE

HASKELL WOLFF

JULY 31, 1998

I was just a dogface, an infantryman. I went in 1944 when I was nineteen years old. I was in the First Army, Ninety-ninth Division, which was sent to England where we trained for a brief period of time. Then we crossed the English Channel. The Normandy Invasion had gone before us. By the time we got there, the American and British forces were fighting in the hedgerows. We proceeded to the Maginot Line, and the Seigfried Line. Then, we were placed in the Ardennes Forest. It was a bitter winter. Our forces were spread thin, from side to side. We didn't expect a counter attack. The 106th Division was on our left flank. We were dug in there for two to three weeks. Since no counter attack was expected, we were permitted to dig in in squad rooms. A foxhole is usually only one or two people, but we had our whole squad in ours. We roofed the place over for protection from the elements. We were prepared to spend the winter there.

Unfortunately, on December 16, just before daybreak, the German artillery started coming in. There was snow on the ground. When we got to peep out, it looked like a checker board. The artillery shells had exploded into the terrain.

I was in a mortar platoon. They taught us something called "searching and patrolling" with your mortar. You search out, and you patrol, say, to the right. Then you patrol back. You continue to search and patrol until you cover a whole area. When I looked out on the snow that morning, it was apparent the Germans had searched and patrolled as far as the eye could see. You could tell because of the black artillery shell marks in the snow. We lost probably thousands of men. That was the morning of the Battle of the Bulge I just described.

In my particular company, about two hundred of us went over together. Seven of us came back. But we lost more than that because we would get in replacements. And, unfortunately, a lot of them were killed, too. All that loss was not death. It might be capture or wounded. That one hundred ninety-three men we lost were lost to the company, but not necessarily by death.

After the Battle of the Bulge, the U.S. forces regrouped as best they could. To the best of my recollection, the 106th Division on our left, had surrendered. That was on December 18. What was left of us pretty much regrouped ourselves. My little group was in a town called Elsenborn, Belgium. It wasn't very far from Bastogne. We were a motley bunch. It was just whoever could get together. A line was re-formed to face the Germans. We pulled back. Then ultimately, we went forward. The Battle of the Bulge lasted about thirty days. It was more or less a holding action. We weren't moving forward and neither were they. I felt Patton was the man who created the end of the Bulge. Now, I'm no historian, I was just lying in a foxhole. But he came from the south with his tanks and he cut off the German Bulge.

We were holed up during and after the Battle of the Bulge, unable to move forward for many days. And the air corps couldn't fly because of the weather. Then one morning the air force showed up, and we were really glad to see them. They started pulverizing the Germans again, and then we could move. We might still be there if it weren't for the air force.

I think a lot of soldiers developed an attitude that if there's not a bullet with your name on it, you won't get it. Of course, we talked to the "man upstairs." I was right next to a lot of death. Some frozen.

When the Bulge was terminated and we started to move forward, we eventually came to the Rhine River. It was believed by us that we would try to cross at Cologne. These were pretty tough days.... It's hard to remember the loss of comrades. In this progress, some guys out on patrol in an armored vehicle came upon a railroad bridge at Remagen, Germany. They crossed without opposition. They radioed back and started pouring all of us into Remagen. I think our division was the first one to cross. That's how we got across the Rhine River. And the push continued.

Haskell Wolff

Next was the Ruhr pocket. We took quite a number of prisoners there. The war was winding down then, maybe not on the Russian front, but we were moving real fast.

I remember that we passed something that was a concentration camp. But we were moving so fast, I didn't go in there. I didn't even know what a concentration camp was. I thought maybe it was a prison. We were barreling forward, but our rear echelon went in and liberated it. They discovered all the gory details. Our division flag now flies in front of the Holocaust Museum in Washington, D.C.

We ended up in Bavaria. I was relaxing in a hay barn when word came down, “The war is over.” Those were good, good words. We hooted and hollered.

We went back to the port of embarkation in France. We received word that we would get to come home for a month. Then we’d report to San Francisco to go to the South Pacific. And those weren’t good words. But before I could leave for San Francisco, we heard that Truman had dropped the bomb.

My hero was my daddy. Patriotism was instilled in me as a child. It meant to do the best you can for your country. I’m afraid it’s lost on some of today’s younger generation. The loss of patriotism gained momentum with the Viet Nam War.

I haven’t delved too much into thinking about how I would want to be remembered, but I hope I will be remembered in a kindly light. Maybe just an old guy with war stories?